Passing PTLLS Assessments

2nd edition

Passing PTLLS Assessments

2nd edition

Ann Gravells

Los Angeles | London | New Delhi
Singapore | Washington DC

Learning Matters
An imprint of SAGE Publications Ltd
1 Oliver's Yard
55 City Road
London EC1Y 1SP

SAGE Publications Inc.
2455 Teller Road
Thousand Oaks, California 91320

SAGE Publications India Pvt Ltd
B 1/I 1 Mohan Cooperative Industrial Area
Mathura Road
New Delhi 110 044

SAGE Publications Asia-Pacific Pte Ltd
3 Chuch Street
#10–04 Samsung Hub
Singapore 049483

© 2012 Ann Gravells

First published in 2010
Reprinted in 2010 (twice)
Reprinted in 2011
Second edition published in 2012
Reprinted in 2013

Apart from any fair dealing for the purposes of research or private study, or criticism or review, as permitted under the Copyright, Design and Patents Act, 1988, this publication may be reproduced, stored or transmitted in any form, or by any means, only with the prior permission in writing of the publishers, or in the case of reprographic reproduction, in accordance with the terms of licences issued by the Copyright Licensing Agency. Enquiries concerning reproduction outside these terms should be sent to the publishers.

Library of Congress Control Number: 2012936242

British Library Cataloguing in Publication Data

A catalogue record for this book is available from the British Library

Editor: Amy Thornton
Development Editor: Jennifer Clark
Production Controller: Chris Marke
Project Management: Deer Park Productions, Tavistock
Marketing Manager: Catherine Slinn
Cover Design: Topics
Typeset by: Pantek Media
Printed by: Bell & Bain Ltd, Glasgow

ISBN: 978 0 85725 870 0
ISBN: 978 0 85725 789 5 (pbk)

CONTENTS

ACKNOWLEDGEMENTS

I would like to thank the following for their support and contributions whilst writing this book:

Peter Adeney, Warwick Andrews, Kathy Beevers, Suzanne Blake, Richard Malthouse and Mel Page.

I would also like to thank my father Bob Gravells for his excellent proof reading skills. Also, my husband Peter Frankish who never complains about the amount of time I spend in the office. And to Jennifer Clark my editor, and Amy Thornton from Learning Matters who are always at the end of the phone when I feel under pressure and need motivation and encouragement.

Every effort has been made to trace the copyright holders and to obtain their permission for the use of copyright material. The publisher and author will gladly receive any information enabling them to rectify any error or omission in subsequent editions.

Ann Gravells
www.anngravells.co.uk

Ann Gravells is a lecturer in teacher training at Bishop Burton College in East Yorkshire and a consultant to The University of Cambridge's Institute of Continuing Education's Assessment Network. She has been teaching since 1983.

Ann is a director of her own company *Ann Gravells Ltd*, an educational consultancy which specialises in teaching, training and quality assurance. She delivers events and courses nationwide.

Ann holds a Masters in Educational Management, a PGCE, a Degree in Education, and a City & Guilds Medal of Excellence for teaching. Ann is a Fellow of the Institute for Learning and holds QTLS status.

She is often asked how her surname should be pronounced. The 'vells' part of Gravells is pronounced like 'bells'.

She is the author of:

- *Achieving your TAQA Assessor and Internal Quality Assurer Award*
- *Delivering Employability Skills in the Lifelong Learning Sector*
- *Passing PTLLS Assessments*
- *Preparing to Teach in the Lifelong Learning Sector*
- *Principles and Practice of Assessment in the Lifelong Learning Sector*
- *What is Teaching in the Lifelong Learning Sector?*

co-author of:

- *Equality and Diversity in the Lifelong Learning Sector*
- *Passing CTLLS Assessments*
- *Planning and Enabling Learning in the Lifelong Learning Sector*

She has edited:

- *Study Skills for PTLLS*

The author welcomes any comments from readers; please contact her via her website.

www.anngravells.co.uk

In this chapter you will learn about:

- the structure of the book and how to use it
- the PTLLS Award
- self assessment activities and guidance for evidencing achievement
- PTLLS assessment methods

The structure of the book and how to use it

The book is designed to help you assess the skills and knowledge you already have, in preparation for your formal assessments. It is not a text book, but a self-assessment book, and should therefore be read in conjunction with an appropriate text book such as *Preparing to Teach in the Lifelong Learning Sector: The New Award* by Ann Gravells.

This book will suit anyone taking the PTLLS Award, whether you are taking a short intensive programme of study, attending a formal programme over a number of days or weeks, or taking a distance, open or blended learning approach.

Chapters 1–12 contain self assessment activities for you to carry out, together with guidance to help you demonstrate and evidence your achievement towards each PTLLS learning outcome. Additional guidance is given towards level 4 achievement. The book is not intended to give you the answers to questions you may be asked in any formal assessments; your responses will be *specific to you*, the *subject* you will teach and the *context* and *environment* in which you teach. The book will, however, guide you through the PTLLS Award learning outcomes with a view to helping you focus upon the requirements of the assessment criteria.

Chapter 13 will help you plan and prepare for your micro-teach session. You will also gain information regarding giving feedback to your peers after their micro-teach sessions, and how to evaluate your own session.

At the end of Chapters 1–12 is an example of a completed assessment grid at level 3 and level 4. These give examples of evidence you could provide for each of the assessment criteria. Evidence can be cross-referenced between the assessment criteria as there is some duplication between the content. The PTLLS Award consists of four units, which can be achieved independently of each other or at the same time.

For the purpose of this book, the generic term *teacher* is used to denote a teacher, trainer, tutor, instructor, facilitator, lecturer, etc. However, your teacher might also assess you and therefore the terms assessor and observer are used in the book to denote this. The generic term *student* is used to denote a learner, student, trainee, candidate, participant, etc. Change is inevitable in education and terminology changes regularly. The term *learner* was used when the PTLLS learning outcomes and assessment criteria were written, however, the term *student* is currently used. You will therefore see the use of both learner and student throughout the chapters.

Appendix 1 contains a list of relevant educational abbreviations and acronyms, and Appendix 2 contains a glossary of terms which relate to the Lifelong Learning Sector.

The index at the back of the book will help you to locate relevant topics quickly.

The PTLLS Award

The Preparing to Teach in the Lifelong Learning Sector (PTLLS) Award is the first step on the teacher training qualification ladder for anyone wanting to teach in the post compulsory education and training sector – known as *the Lifelong Learning Sector*. You do not need to be in a teaching role or have students of your own to take the Award. It is ideal if you just want to find out what it's like to teach without becoming a teacher. Part of the Award requires you to deliver a short session to your peers if you are pre-service (i.e. not yet teaching), or to your current students if you are in-service (i.e. currently teaching). You can usually decide on the subject for this, which might be based on your current job role or a skill or hobby.

The PTLLS Award is made up of the following four units available at both level 3 and 4 on the Qualifications and Credit Framework (QCF) or their *accepted alternatives*.

- Roles, responsibilities and relationships in lifelong learning.

- Understanding inclusive learning and teaching in lifelong learning.

- Using inclusive learning and teaching approaches in lifelong learning.

- Principles of assessment in lifelong learning.

This book focuses upon the assessment criteria of the four units above. There are *accepted alternatives* to those listed which come from the Learning and Development suite of qualifications.

The accepted alternative units are:

- Facilitate learning and development for individuals.

- Facilitate learning and development in groups.

- Manage learning and development in groups.

- Understanding the principles and practices of assessment.

If you already hold one of the above units, you might be able to claim credit for it towards one of the four PTLLS units. There are rules as to which ones can be substituted, known as *rules of combination*. You will need to discuss this with your assessor and provide evidence of achievement, for example, your certificate.

The PTLLS Award is 12 credits on the QCF, one credit equals approximately 10 hours of learning. This means a total of 120 hours of learning are required to achieve the Award. This time will be a mixture of contact time with a teacher/assessor and non-contact time for self study and assessment work.

The Award is offered at two levels to differentiate for people's abilities. The content is the same at both level 3 and level 4; the difference in level is expressed through the skills and knowledge required for achievement. For example, if you are taking level 3 you will *explain* how or why you do something, at level 4 you will *analyse* how or why you do it. Your teacher will be able to give you guidance regarding the levels and the amount of work you will need to submit.

All new teachers (who teach on funded programmes in England) in the Lifelong Learning Sector must undertake the Preparing to Teach in the Lifelong Learning Sector (PTLLS) Award at the beginning of their career.

This can be as a discrete award or embedded in the Certificate in Teaching in the Lifelong Learning Sector (CTLLS) or the Diploma in Teaching in the Lifelong Learning Sector (DTLLS) qualifications. Some Higher Education Institutions still use the term *Certificate in Education (Cert Ed)*, even though the content is the same as the Diploma. There is also a *Professional Graduate Certificate in Education* and a *Postgraduate Certificate in Education (PGCE)*, which again cover the same content as DTLLS but are offered at higher levels. These programmes sometimes integrate the PTLLS units within other units.

The book was written prior to the Lord Lingfield Interim Report *Professionalism in Further Education* (2012). There may have been some changes to the requirements for teachers in the Lifelong Learning Sector as a result of the subsequent report which was due after this book was published.

Taking the PTLLS Award

To start the process of achieving your PTLLS Award, you will need to enrol at a training organisation, college or other establishment that offers it. If you are currently teaching (in-service), your employer might inform you where you can take it and might also fund it for you. If you are not yet teaching (pre-service), you will need to find out where the PTLLS Award is offered and apply for a place. A quick search via the internet or a phone call to your local training provider or college will soon locate these. You might be interviewed (in person or on the telephone) and/or have to complete an application form (paper based or electronic). At this stage it would be useful to ask any questions or discuss any concerns you might have prior to commencing. You should also undertake an initial assessment, which might involve completing a form or having a discussion with your teacher. This will ascertain if you have any particular learning needs, for example with literacy or numeracy, and if you need help with study skills. You should always be honest when asked so that you can be appropriately supported through your learning experience.

Depending upon where you have enrolled, the training provider will explain how the programme will be delivered and assessed. It might be by attending formal sessions on a weekly or daily basis at a certain venue, or a mix of attending sessions combined with study packs. Other approaches might involve visiting you in your workplace, supporting you on a one-to-one basis, or a blended learning approach, for example, completing activities online via the internet, or working at home with occasional attendance at group sessions.

You will have a designated teacher and assessor at the training organisation who will give you ongoing support, guidance and feedback throughout your time taking the Award. If you don't pass any assessments first time, you should be given the opportunity to discuss them with your assessor and have another attempt. The activities in this book will help you understand the PTLLS Award criteria and prepare you for the assessments, they are not a substitute for any formal assessments you will be given. If you are an in-service teacher, you should be assigned a *mentor*. This is someone, preferably in the same organisation and subject area as yourself, who should be able to give you ongoing help, support and advice.

As you work through the units' requirements you will be informed regularly of your progress by your assessor and you should have the opportunity to discuss any issues or concerns. The work you produce towards achieving the assessment criteria of the PTLLS units will be formally assessed and you will receive feedback.

A sample of your work might be *internally* and/or *externally quality assured*. Internal quality assurance means someone else who works in the same organisation where you are taking the PTLLS Award will sample aspects of the assessment process. This is to ensure you have been assessed fairly and that your work has met the qualification standards. External quality assurance means someone from the Awarding Organisation who issues your certificate might also sample the assessment and internal quality assurance process.

Self assessment activities and guidance for evidencing achievement

As you progress through your programme of study, you can work through the self assessment activities in Chapters 1–12. Each chapter relates to one of the twelve PTLLS learning outcomes. Responding to these activities will help you focus upon the assessment criteria and guide you towards evidencing the PTLLS Award learning outcomes.

As you work through the self assessment activities, make sure your responses are *specific to you* and the *subject* you will teach. You should state the *context* and *environment* in which you will teach. Examples of the context could be:

- adult and community learning
- emergency, public and uniformed services

- further education college

- Ministry of Defence/Armed Forces

- offender learning

- sixth form and specialist colleges

- training organisation

- voluntary or private sector

- work-based learning

Examples of the environment include classrooms, community halls, out-door spaces, training rooms, workshops, the workplace, etc.

If you are currently teaching, you could explain the documentation you use at work along with the relevant policies, procedures and guidelines you follow. You could also produce a case study which puts theory into practice.

Once you have completed the activities in the first part of the chapter, check your responses with the guidance in the second part of the chapter. There are also examples of completed assessment grids at the end of each chapter which give you guidance as to what you could submit as evidence of achievement.

PTLLS assessment methods

Each Awarding Organisation will design their own assessment strategy for the PTLLS Award, therefore the methods may vary depending upon who you are registered with. A few of the assessment methods are explained here. If you are in any doubt as to how you will be assessed, you will need to talk to your PTLLS teacher.

Assessment grids and checklists

The Awarding Organisation you are registered with may have produced a grid or a checklist which contains all the PTLLS assessment criteria for each of the four units. Either you or your assessor will complete these to show how you have achieved them. Your supporting evidence, for example, written statements, session plans, etc. (often called *product evidence*), should clearly demonstrate how you have met the criteria at the level you aim to achieve. Often, more than one assessment criteria can be achieved by the use of a well-written statement or good piece of quality evidence.

It is also possible to meet the requirements of several assessment criteria from different units at the same time. If this is the case, you will be able to cross-reference your evidence rather than duplicate it. For example, your micro-teach session plan and teaching materials might demonstrate aspects from all four units.

Your supporting evidence could be kept in a portfolio which can be either electronic or manual. Examples of completed assessment grids for each learning outcome are at the end of Chapters 1–12.

Assignments

These will ensure that all the assessment criteria can be met through various tasks or activities which will cover both theory and practice. They might not be in the same order as the PTLLS Award learning outcomes; however, you should be able to complete all the requirements as you progress through your programme of study. There might be several theory or practical tasks or activities for you to complete, which could include group discussions, presentations, essays and worksheets with time for self-reflection, feedback and evaluation of progress. Some written tasks and essays might have word counts to ensure you remain focused and specific with your responses, and all will have deadline dates for submission. You will usually have to word process your work in a professional font; however, if it is acceptable for you to handwrite your responses, make sure your writing is legible and neatly written. Your teacher will give you guidance as to how to present your work. Always check your spelling, grammar, punctuation and sentence structure. Try not to rely on your computer to check things for you as it doesn't always realise the context within which you are writing. If you cannot keep to a submission date for any reason, make sure you discuss this with your teacher.

Referencing

If you are working at level 4, you might be asked to reference your work to relevant texts, journals, websites, etc. However, it is also good practice to do this at level 3. For example, if you are describing ground rules, you could state:

> Ground rules should be agreed at the start of a new programme. *Ground rules are boundaries, rules and conditions within which students can safely work and learn* (Gravells, 2012: 91). It is important to establish these early to ensure the programme runs smoothly. If students do not feel safe, they might not return again, or their learning could be affected.

Any quote you insert within your text should be in *italics* or within quotation marks. The name of the author, the year of publication of the book and the page number should be in brackets directly afterwards. At the end of your work, you should have a reference list giving the full details of the book you have quoted from. For example:

Gravells, A (2012) *Preparing to Teach in the Lifelong Learning Sector: The New Award.* London: Learning Matters.

Before inserting a quote, make sure you understand what it means and how it will fit within your writing. It could be that you agree with what the author said and it supports what you are saying, or it could be that you totally disagree with it. If so, explain why you disagree and state what you would do differently. You need to state what you think, or what your point of view is. Throughout your writing, you should refer to different sources and authors where applicable. The organisation you are taking the PTLLS programme with should be able to give you advice regarding using quotes and referencing your work.

It is advisable to use a range of sources to develop your knowledge and understanding. Reading more than one book will help you to gain the perspectives of different authors. You don't have to read the full books, you can just locate relevant topics by using the index at the back of the book. The text book *Study Skills for PTLLS* (2nd Edn) by Jacklyn Williams (2012) will help you with your referencing skills.

Observation

At some point, you will be observed delivering a session, after the observation you will receive feedback. A visual recording might be made of your session which you can view in your own time. This will enable you to see things you weren't aware of, for example, saying 'erm' or not using much eye contact with students. You need to consider these points and the feedback received when completing your self-evaluation. You will also observe your peers and have the opportunity to give them feedback.

Whilst you are taking the PTLLS Award you may find it useful to arrange to observe your mentor if you are in-service, or a teacher in the same subject area as yourself if you are pre-service. This will help you to see how they plan, prepare, deliver, assess and evaluate their session, giving you some useful ideas.

Online assessments

You will either e-mail your work to your assessor or upload it to a learning portal via a website. If you are taking the PTLLS Award totally via an online programme, you might not meet the person who will give you feedback concerning your work. You need to stay in touch regularly and communicate any issues or concerns to them. You will still have to deliver a session and be observed doing this.

Online assessment can include *formative* assessment, i.e. obtaining feedback from your assessor regarding a draft submission of your work. This feedback will help confirm if you are making good progress or advise you of areas you need to improve. You could then upload your completed work for *summative* assessment when you have finalised it.

Portfolio of evidence

You will usually collect *evidence*, i.e. proof of your achievements, which could be electronic (for example, word processed), or manual (for example, documents placed in a ring binder or folder). This is known as a portfolio and will contain all the evidence you have produced to fulfil the assessment criteria for each learning outcome of the PTLLS Award. When producing this evidence consider quality not quantity. Your assessor's observation and feedback notes should also be included as proof of your achievements. If you have re-done any work, you will need to include your original and your revised work.

Professional discussion

A professional discussion is a conversation with your assessor in which you will justify how you have achieved the requirements of the PTLLS Award. Your assessor might explore your knowledge and understanding of the teaching role to ensure you have met the assessment criteria. Having a professional discussion with your assessor is a good way to demonstrate how you have met the criteria if you are having difficulty expressing yourself through written work.

A professional discussion can be used as a *holistic* assessment method, meaning several criteria can be assessed at the same time. Your assessor will prompt you to explain how you have met the requirements and ask to see documentation which confirms this. They will take notes during the discussion and might also make a recording of your conversation if appropriate, either visual or aural, which can be kept as evidence of your achievement. Prior to the professional discussion taking place, you should agree with your assessor the nature of the conversation to enable you to prepare in advance. You may need to bring along examples of teaching materials you have prepared and used. When you are having the professional discussion try and remain focused, don't digress but be specific with your responses when asked a question. At the end of the discussion, your assessor should confirm which assessment criteria you have achieved, and which you still need to work towards.

Questions – written and oral

You may need to produce answers to written questions which will be based around the assessment criteria. See the section on *assignments* for more information.

You might also be asked oral questions by your assessor who will note down your responses or record your conversation. If you have answered a written question and met most but not all of the assessment criteria, your assessor might ask some oral questions to ensure you have the relevant skills and knowledge.

Reflective learning journal

Writing a reflective learning journal throughout your programme of study will help you focus upon your learning and development, enabling you to put theory into practice. You might be given a pro-forma to complete or you could write in a diary or a notebook or use a word processor. When you write, make sure your work is legible as your assessor will need to read and understand it. Try and reflect upon your experiences by analysing as well as describing them and be as specific as possible as to how your experiences have met the PTLLS Award assessment criteria. You could annotate your writing with the assessment criteria numbers such as 1.1, 1.2, etc to show which criteria you feel you have achieved. Don't just write a chronological account of events, consider what worked well, or didn't work, and how you could do something differently given the opportunity. If you are working at level 4, you could reference your work to reflective theories to demonstrate how you have put theory into practice. For example:

'Today I taught a group of 15 students who were very disruptive. I introduced the topic at the beginning and most of them were talking over me. I tried shouting but this didn't have any effect. What I should have done was remain silent straight away until all the students looked at me. This is based on Schön D (1983) – reflection in action. This would have gained their attention and

enabled me to remind them of the ground rules regarding disruption. Next time I will display the ground rules on the wall and remind the group of these before we commence, which is based on Schön – reflection on action.'

Reflection should become a part of your everyday activities and enable you to look at things in detail that you perhaps would not ordinarily do. There may be events you would not want to change or improve if you felt they went well. If this is the case, reflect as to *why* they went well and use similar situations in future sessions. As you become more experienced at reflective writing, you will see how you can make improvements to benefit your students.

Self-evaluation record and action plan

This is a pro-forma for you to complete at the end of your teaching session. Your assessor might also complete a marking grid and observation record to ensure you have met the PTLLS Award requirements. Your responses and evidence should clearly demonstrate how you have met the criteria at the level you wish to achieve. The action plan will help you focus upon the skills, knowledge and understanding required for your personal development. You need to focus upon what you have learnt and how you have put this into practice, relating this to the skills, knowledge and understanding required for your development.

Summary

In this chapter you have learnt about:

- the structure of the book and how to use it
- the PTLLS Award
- self assessment activities and guidance for evidencing achievement
- PTLLS assessment methods

Theory focus

References and further information

Gravells, A (2012) *Preparing to Teach in the Lifelong Learning Sector: The New Award* (5th Edn). London: Learning Matters.

Gravells, A (2011) *Principles and Practice of Assessment in the Lifelong Learning Sector* (2nd Edn). Exeter: Learning Matters.

Lingfield Lord (2012) *Professionalism in Further Education* London Dept. for Business, Innovation and skills.

LLUK (2006) *New overarching professional standards for teachers, tutors and trainers in the Lifelong Learning Sector.* London: Skills for Business.

Reece, I and Walker, S (2008) *Teaching Training and Learning: a practical guide* (6th Edn). Tyne & Wear: Business Education Publishers Ltd.

Schön, D (1983) *The Reflective Practitioner.* San Francisco, CA: Jossey-Bass.

Wallace, S (2011) *Teaching, Tutoring and Training in the Lifelong Learning Sector* (4th Edn). Exeter: Learning Matters.

Williams, J (2012) *Study Skills for PTLLS* (2nd Edn). London: Learning Matters.

Websites

Awarding Organisations – www.ofqual.gov.uk/for-awarding-organisations

Institute for Learning – www.ifl.ac.uk

Learning and Skills Improvement Service – www.lsis.org.uk

Qualifications and Credit Framework shortcut – http://tinyurl.com/447bgy2

Scottish Credit and Qualifications Framework – www.scqf.org.uk

CHAPTER 1
UNDERSTAND OWN ROLE AND RESPONSIBILITIES IN LIFELONG LEARNING

This chapter is in two parts. The first part: *Self assessment activities*, contains questions and activities which relate to the first learning outcome of the PTLLS unit *Roles, responsibilities and relationships in lifelong learning*.

The assessment criteria for each level are shown in boxes and are followed by questions and activities for you to carry out. Ensure your responses are *specific to you*, the *subject* you will teach and the *context* and *environment* in which you will teach.

After completing the activities, check your responses with the second part: *Guidance for evidencing achievement*. This guidance is not intended to give you the answers to questions you may be asked in any formal assessments; however, it will help you focus your responses towards meeting the PTLLS assessment criteria.

At the end of each chapter is an example of a completed assessment grid at level 3 and level 4. These give examples of evidence you could provide towards the assessment criteria. Evidence can be cross-referenced between units and assessment criteria if it meets the requirements.

Self assessment activities

Level 3 – 1.1 Summarise key aspects of legislation, regulatory requirements and codes of practice relating to own role and responsibilities

Level 4 – 1.1 Summarise key aspects of legislation, regulatory requirements and codes of practice relating to own role and responsibilities

Q1 What legislation, regulatory requirements and codes of practice must you follow to teach your subject?

Q2 Summarise the key aspects of these.

> Level 3 – 1.2 Explain own responsibilities for promoting equality and valuing diversity
>
> Level 4 – 1.2 Analyse own responsibilities for promoting equality and valuing diversity

Q3 What do the terms equality and diversity mean?

Q4 Explain (level 3) or analyse (level 4) what you consider your responsibilities to be in promoting equality and valuing diversity.

> Level 3 – 1.3 Explain own role and responsibilities in lifelong learning
>
> Level 4 – 1.3 Evaluate own role and responsibilities in lifelong learning

Q5 Explain (level 3) or evaluate (level 4) what you consider your role as a teacher to be.

Q6 Explain (level 3) or evaluate (level 4) your responsibilities as a teacher.

> Level 3 – 1.4 Explain own role and responsibilities in identifying and meeting the needs of learners
>
> Level 4 – 1.4 Review own role and responsibilities in identifying and meeting the needs of learners

Q7 How can you identify the needs of students. Give some examples.

Q8 Explain (level 3) or review (level 4) how you can meet these needs.

Guidance for evidencing achievement

Level 3 – 1.1 Summarise key aspects of legislation, regulatory requirements and codes of practice relating to own role and responsibilities

Level 4 – 1.1 Summarise key aspects of legislation, regulatory requirements and codes of practice relating to own role and responsibilities

Q1 What legislation, regulatory requirements and codes of practice must you follow to teach your subject?

These will differ depending upon your subject, the context and environment within which you teach, however, your response could include a generic list such as:

- Awarding Organisation guidelines for delivering and assessing your subject
- Copyright Designs and Patents Act (1988)
- Criminal Records Bureau (CRB) clearance
- Data Protection Act (2003)
- Equality Act (2010)
- Health and Safety at Work etc Act (1974)
- Inspection requirements (Ofsted, etc)
- Institute for Learning (IfL) Code of Professional Practice (2008)
- Organisational guidelines such as dress and timekeeping
- Organisational policies and procedures such as appeals, complaints and risk assessments
- Safeguarding Vulnerable Groups Act (2006)
- The Further Education Teachers' Qualifications (England) Regulations (2007) (QTLS/ATLS status)

You could also list specific requirements which are relevant to your subject. For example, the Control of Substances Hazardous to Health (COSHH) Regulations (2002) if you work with hazardous materials, the Display Screen Regulations (1992) if you work with computers, or Food Hygiene Regulations (2006) if you work in catering. There might be requirements relevant to external bodies such as a Sector Skills Council (SSC). SSCs are responsible for creating the standards which are used as a basis for qualifications.

At level 4 you could also give details of where the information relating to the above can be accessed, for example, your organisation's intranet, websites or a library, etc. You should also use quotes from relevant text books or organisational policies to support your response, for instance, those relating to codes of practice such as disciplinary, conduct, dress and time-keeping, etc.

Q2 Summarise the key aspects of these.

One example is summarised below, you will need to research and summarise the key aspects of the others you have referred to in your previous response.

The Health and Safety at Work etc Act (1974). This addresses the health and safety of employers and employees within the working environment and outlines the legal responsibilities of individuals for health and safety issues. It may be necessary to carry out certain risk assessments, for example, before a cookery session it may be necessary to assess any specific needs of the students in relation to the environment where the teaching will take place, taking into consideration possible dangers such as sharp knives and hot ovens.

At level 4 you will need to go into greater detail. You could perhaps research your organisation's Health and Safety policies and procedures and explain what you would do if a situation occurred with a student. You could also state who is responsible for health and safety, and find out what was amended when the policy was last reviewed.

> Level 3 – 1.2 Explain own responsibilities for promoting equality and valuing diversity
>
> Level 4 – 1.2 Analyse own responsibilities for promoting equality and valuing diversity

Q3 What do the terms equality and diversity mean?

Equality is about the rights of students to have access to, attend, and participate in their chosen learning experience. This should be regardless of ability and/or circumstances. *Diversity* is about valuing and respecting the differences in students, regardless of ability and/or circumstances, or any other individual characteristics they may have.

At level 4 you could relate your response to quotes from text books. For example, *You must not allow any form of discrimination in your classroom or learning situation. Not only is it morally wrong, it is likely to be illegal* (Reece and Walker, 2007: 295). You could then discuss this quote as to how you would ensure discrimination does not take place. You could also relate your response to equality of opportunity. This is a concept underpinned by The Equality Act (2010) to provide relevant and appropriate access for the participation, development and advancement of all individuals and groups. *In the past, equality has often been described as everyone being the same or having the same opportunities. Nowadays, it can be described as everyone being different, but having equal rights* (Gravells, 2012: 53, 54).

Q4 Explain (level 3) or analyse (level 4) what you consider your responsibilities to be in promoting equality and valuing diversity.

Your response could explain your considerations, for example, responsibilities should include promoting positive behaviour, diversity and inclusion throughout the teaching and learning process. You should also challenge prejudice, discrimination and stereotyping as it occurs. Incorporating activities based around equality and diversity could help with your students' understanding, for example, discussions based around different faiths and religions. Using naturally occurring opportunities to explore aspects such as Ramadan or Chinese New Year when they occur will also help your students appreciate and value diversity. You might have students of different levels within your group; setting different tasks and targets might help rather than expecting everyone to achieve the same tasks at the same time.

At level 4 you could analyse your responsibilities, for example, how you could ensure all students have access to learning, not only physical access, but ensuring teaching and learning materials are suitable and accessible to all students. For example, producing resources in different formats i.e. hard copy and/or electronic. This will be based on your students' needs which you will have identified beforehand. You could state how you will ensure the nine protected characteristics of The Equality Act (2010) are met through the policies and procedures of your organisation. They are:

- age

- disability

- gender

- gender identify

- race

- religion and belief

- sexual orientation

- marriage and civil partnership

- maternity and pregnancy

You could also expand on the Act by discussing how it provides rights for people not to be directly discriminated against or harassed because they have an association with a disabled person or because they are wrongly perceived as disabled. You could also relate your response to relevant quotes from text books.

Level 3 – 1.3 Explain own role and responsibilities in lifelong learning

Level 4 – 1.3 Evaluate own role and responsibilities in lifelong learning

---

Q5 Explain (level 3) or evaluate (level 4) what you consider your role as a teacher to be.

Your response could explain that primarily your role is to help your students achieve their chosen programme. This will be by using various teaching and learning approaches and taking individual needs into account. You could explain that one of your roles is to identify learner needs which include:

- arranging suitable initial assessments

- carrying out interviews

- identifying any barriers or challenges to learning

- identifying any particular student, self and organisational needs.

You could then explain your other roles.

At level 4 you will need to evaluate the roles you have stated in more detail. This could be by identifying the advantages and limitations of what you consider your role will involve. For example, *arranging suitable initial assessments* – an advantage would be to ascertain the current skills and knowledge of students to agree a suitable learning plan. A limitation would be if the initial assessment was carried out too late, the student could be working towards an unsuitable programme or level.

You could also refer to theorists within your response such as Fleming's (2005) Learning Styles or Kolb's (1984) Experiential Learning Cycle, and evaluate how these would impact upon your role as a teacher. Students develop skills, knowledge and attitudes in different ways, therefore you could evaluate how this would occur in your particular subject area.

Q6 Explain (level 3) or evaluate (level 4) your responsibilities as a teacher.

Your response could be linked to the roles which you identified in Q5.

For example, your responsibilities for *carrying out interviews* could include:

- planning a suitable date and time
- conveying this to all concerned
- booking an appropriate room
- having all necessary documentation ready
- liaising with others as necessary
- maintaining records.

Your response could then explain how you would carry out each of the aspects you have listed.

At level 4 you will need to evaluate how your stated responsibilities impact upon your role and your students. For example, what would happen if you didn't carry out your responsibilities adequately? You could also refer to codes of practice which you should follow, such as the Institute for Learning's (IfL) Code of Professional Practice (2008), which covers the following areas:

- professional integrity
- respect
- reasonable care

- professional practice

- criminal offence disclosure

- responsibility during Institute investigations

- responsibility

You could cross-reference your response to Q2 (assessment criteria 1.1) regarding the IfL Code of Professional Practice if you mentioned this previously.

> Level 3 – 1.4 Explain own role and responsibilities in identifying and meeting the needs of learners
>
> Level 4 – 1.4 Review own role and responsibilities in identifying and meeting the needs of learners

Q7 How can you identify the needs of students. Give some examples.

Your response could state the roles and responsibilities you have which enable you to identify the needs of your students. For example, your role would be to arrange for suitable initial assessments to take place. Your responsibility would be to ensure they are carried out at a suitable time and place and that the results are used effectively. Student needs can be ascertained prior to commencement, as part of the initial assessment process, during discussions at the interview stage, or tutorials part way through the programme.

Some examples of the needs of students might include:

- dyslexia

- English as a second language

- financial, health and personal problems

- physical or mental disabilities

- study skills concerns

If you are not an expert with any of these you should refer your students to an appropriate specialist. You might also encounter students who have achieved part of the qualification elsewhere and who therefore will not need to repeat some aspects of the programme. You could state how you would deal with this, for example, they could still attend the programme, but not be reassessed for the aspects they have already achieved elsewhere.

At level 4, you could review the different methods which can be used to identify student needs, for example, a paper-based questionnaire versus an online questionnaire. You could also review the systems used at your organisation and state how effective they are, or what changes you would recommend and why.

Q8 Explain (level 3) or review (level 4) how you can meet these needs.

Your response could explain how you can meet the needs you have identified in your response to Q7. Needs can include supporting a student who has dyslexia, for example *by photocopying handouts onto different coloured paper* (Wilson, 2008: 238). You can also signpost students to other programmes, for example, literacy and numeracy, or if applicable you could make adjustments to the learning environment. Addressing student needs can also be met by identifying their learning styles. If students have access to the internet, a quick and easy questionnaire can be completed at www.vark-learn.com to ascertain whether they are visual, aural, read/write or kinaesthetic (VARK). This can be completed prior to or during the beginning of a programme. The results of these will help plan for effective learning to take place. For example, if the group are mainly kinaesthetic it would be inappropriate to use theoretical materials for most of the time. There are other needs a student may have which you might have experienced and could explain.

At level 4 you could respond in more detail, reviewing the needs you have identified and referring to relevant texts. For example, if you are reviewing how students' basic needs must be met for learning to be effective, you could discuss relevant theorists such as Maslow's Hierarchy of Needs (1962) as stated in Reece and Walker (2007: 77): *The physical (comfort requirements) can be met by providing adequate breaks, ensuring comfort, arranging seats according to needs and being alert to heating and ventilation requirements.* You could then review how you would ensure this would happen within the learning environment. You could discuss other theorists such as Herzberg (1991) as stated in Gravells and Simpson (2010: 111): *Motivation needs include factors which allow for: achievement, responsibility, recognition, advancement and challenge. Herzberg suggests that these factors are the ones which encourage people to strive to do well, and motivate them to do their best.*

Comparing these two theorists would demonstrate your understanding of them. If you have mentioned learning styles in your previous response, you could compare and contrast Fleming's (2005) visual, aural, read/write and kinesthetic with Honey and Mumford's (1992) activist, pragmatist, theorist and reflector as in Gravells (2012). You could also review the advantages and disadvantages of electronic versus paper-based questionnaires.

Theory focus

References and further information

Avis, J, Fisher, R and Thompson, R (2011) *Teaching in Lifelong Learning: A Guide To Theory And Practice*. Oxford: Oxford University Press.

Fleming, N (2005) *Teaching and Learning Styles: VARK Strategies*. Honolulu; Honolulu Community College.

Gravells, A (2012) *Preparing to Teach in the Lifelong Learning Sector: The New Award* (5th Edn). London: Learning Matters.

Gravells, A and Simpson, S (2012) *Equality and Diversity in the Lifelong Learning Sector* (2nd Edn). London: Learning Matters.

Gravells, A and Simpson, S (2010) *Planning and Enabling Learning in the Lifelong Learning Sector* (2nd Edn). Exeter: Learning Matters.

IfL (2008) *Code of Professional Practice*. London: Institute for Learning.

Kolb, DA (1984) *Experiential Learning: Experience as the Source of Learning and Development*. New Jersey: Prentice-Hall.

Reece, I and Walker, S (2007) *Teaching, Training and Learning: A Practical Guide* (6th Edn). Tyne & Wear: Business Education Publishers.

Wallace, S (2011) *Teaching, Tutoring and Training in the Lifelong Learning Sector* (4th Edn). Exeter: Learning Matters.

Williams, J (2012) *Study Skills for PTLLS* (2nd Edn). London: Learning Matters.

Wilson, L (2008) *Practical Teaching: A Guide to PTLLS and CTLLS*. London: Cengage Learning.

Websites

Alliance of Sector Skills Councils – www.sscalliance.org

Copyright Designs and Patents Act (1988) – http://www.opsi.gov.uk/acts/acts1988/UKpga_19880048_en_1.htm

Control of Substances Hazardous to Health (COSHH) – http://www.hse.gov.uk/COSHH/index.htm

Criminal Records Bureau (CRB) – www.crb.gov.uk

Data Protection Act (2003) – http://regulatorylaw.co.uk/Data_Protection_Act_2003.html

Display Screen Regulations (1992) – http://www.opsi.gov.uk/si/si1992/Uksi_19922792_en_1.htm

Equality Act (2010) – http://www.homeoffice.gov.uk/equalities/equality-act/

Equality & Diversity Forum – www.edf.org.uk

Fleming's Learning Styles – www.vark-learn.com

Health & Safety at Work etc Act (1974) – http://www.hse.gov.uk/legislation/hswa.htm

Institute for Learning – www.ifl.ac.uk

Safeguarding Vulnerable Groups Act (2006) – http://www.opsi.gov.uk/ACTS/acts2006/ukpga_20060047_en_1

The Further Education Teachers' Qualifications (England) Regulations (2007) – http://www.opsi.gov.uk/si/si2007/uksi_20072264_en_1

Theories of learning – www.learningandteaching.info/learning/

UNIT TITLE: Roles, responsibilities and relationships in lifelong learning
LEVEL 3

Learning Outcomes The learner will:	Assessment Criteria The learner can:		Example evidence
1. Understand own role and responsibilities in lifelong learning	1.1	Summarise key aspects of legislation, regulatory requirements and codes of practice relating to own role and responsibilities	A list of legislation, regulatory requirements and codes of practice relevant to your role and responsibilities with the key aspects of each summarised.
	1.2	Explain own responsibilities for equality and valuing diversity	An explanation of what equality and diversity mean, along with examples of your responsibilities towards meeting them.
	1.3	Explain own role and responsibilities in lifelong learning	An explanation of the roles and responsibilities of a teacher in the Lifelong Learning Sector. Job description and curriculum vitae if you are currently in a teaching role.
	1.4	Explain own role and responsibilities in identifying and meeting the needs of learners	A list of needs which your students might have. An explanation of how you will identify and meet these needs, based on your roles and responsibilities as a teacher.

UNIT TITLE: Roles, responsibilities and relationships in lifelong learning
LEVEL 4

Learning Outcomes The learner will:	Assessment Criteria The learner can:		Example evidence
1. Understand own role and responsibilities in lifelong learning	1.1	Summarise key aspects of legislation, regulatory requirements and codes of practice relating to own role and responsibilities	A report summarising legislation, regulatory requirements and codes of practice relevant to your role and responsibilities with the key aspects of each summarised. A statement of how these will impact upon your role. A list of relevant websites and where to access information e.g. names of staff in your organisation who are responsible for policies and procedures.
	1.2	Analyse own responsibilities for promoting equality and valuing diversity	An analysis of what equality and diversity mean, along with examples of your responsibilities towards meeting them in different situations. A reflection of how these examples impact upon your job role. A summary of relevant Equality and Diversity legislation, organisational policies and procedures. A list of relevant websites and documents relating to equality and diversity.
	1.3	Evaluate own role and responsibilities in lifelong learning	An evaluation of the roles and responsibilities of a teacher. A detailed evaluation of the identified roles and responsibilities. Job description and curriculum vitae if you are currently in a teaching role which highlights your teaching responsibilities. An evaluation of relevant codes of practice stating how they impact upon your role.
	1.4	Review own role and responsibilities in identifying and meeting the needs of learners	A list of needs which your students might have. A detailed review of how you will identify and meet these needs, based on your roles and responsibilities as a teacher. A comparison of relevant motivation theories.

25

CHAPTER 2
UNDERSTAND THE RELATIONSHIPS BETWEEN TEACHERS AND OTHER PROFESSIONALS IN LIFELONG LEARNING

This chapter is in two parts. The first part: *Self assessment activities*, contains questions and activities which relate to the second learning outcome of the PTLLS unit *Roles, responsibilities and relationships in lifelong learning*.

The assessment criteria for each level are shown in boxes and are followed by questions and activities for you to carry out. Ensure your responses are *specific to you*, the *subject* you will teach and the *context* and *environment* in which you will teach.

After completing the activities and questions, check your responses with the second part: *Guidance for evidencing achievement*. This guidance is not intended to give you the answers to questions you may be asked in any formal assessments; however, it will help you focus your responses towards meeting the PTLLS assessment criteria.

At the end of each chapter is an example of a completed assessment grid at level 3 and level 4. These give examples of evidence you could provide towards the assessment criteria. Evidence can be cross-referenced between units and assessment criteria if it meets the requirements.

Self assessment activities

Level 3 – 2.1 Explain the boundaries between the teaching role and other professional roles

Level 4 – 2.1 Analyse the boundaries between the teaching role and other professional roles

Q9 List the boundaries you might encounter as a teacher in the Lifelong Learning Sector.

Q10 Explain (level 3) or analyse (level 4) the boundaries between the teaching role and other professional roles.

Level 3 – 2.2 Describe points of referral to meet the needs of learners

Level 4 – 2.2 Review points of referral to meet the needs of learners

Q11 Create a list of what you consider the potential needs of students to be.

Q12 Describe (level 3) or review (level 4) points of referral to meet these needs.

Level 3 – 2.3 Summarise own responsibilities in relation to other professionals

Level 4 – 2.3 Evaluate own responsibilities in relation to other professionals

Q13 What are your responsibilities in relation to other professionals?

Q14 Summarise (level 3) or evaluate (level 4) these responsibilities.

Guidance for evidencing achievement

> Level 3 – 2.1 Explain the boundaries between the teaching role and other professional roles
>
> Level 4 – 2.1 Analyse the boundaries between the teaching role and other professional roles

Q9 List the boundaries you might encounter as a teacher in the Lifelong Learning Sector.

Your response could list boundaries such as:

- broken or faulty equipment
- deadlines and targets
- demands from managers
- funding constraints
- lack of own specialist knowledge or skills
- lack of resources
- personal issues and professional concerns
- unmotivated or reluctant students

At level 4 you could state why the boundaries you have listed might have a negative impact upon your role, and give examples.

Q10 Explain (level 3) or analyse (level 4) the boundaries between the teaching role and other professional roles.

Your response could explain how the boundaries you have listed in Q9 impact upon your teaching role and the other professional roles you hold. For example, *demands from managers* could include the pressure to complete certain administration requirements, which you might not consider a priority. The impact could be that they were not completed in time and your manager was unable to finish a report, or you did complete them in time but to the detriment of your other teaching roles. Often, teachers carry out a lot of their role in their own time, such as preparation and marking to ensure their session runs smoothly.

Boundaries are all about knowing your own limits and knowing what your professional role involves, for example, you might telephone a student if they have been absent, but making several calls would be inappropriate. You should remain professional at all times and not get personally involved, for example, not joining students' social networking sites if asked. You should avoid touching students inappropriately or giving extra support to some students and not others. You need to remain in control, be fair and ethical with all your students and don't demonstrate any favouritism towards particular students.

At level 4 you will need to analyse the boundaries you listed in Q9 and state what you would or would not do in specific circumstances. You need to know what your teaching role involves and not overstep your responsibilities. For example, if you had a student who was experiencing financial problems you would advise them to seek specialist help. You would not discuss their income and expenditure with them or advise them to take out a loan as this is not part of your teaching or professional role. Some organisations have specialist staff who are able to advise and support students with a wide variety of welfare issues.

You could analyse the impact that attending meetings has upon your role. For example, it could be time consuming, it might be on a day or time you are not normally working but are expected to attend. There might be several negative aspects to attending, but the positive aspects might outweigh these, for example, the knowledge you can gain and/or the people you can network with. Always remember you are representing your department or organisation at any meetings, and must act professionally at all times.

You could also discuss quotes from relevant texts, for example, *Professionalism requires us to maintain appropriate standards and fulfill our responsibilities to learners, institutions and colleagues* (Francis and Gould, 2009: 10). You could explore how this is achieved, and relate your response to the behaviour aspects of the Institute for Learning's (IfL) Code of Professional Practice (2008).

> Level 3 – 2.2 Describe points of referral to meet the needs of learners
>
> Level 4 – 2.2 Review points of referral to meet the needs of learners

Q11 Create a list of what you consider the potential needs of students to be.

Your response could list potential needs of students such as:

- fear of information technology

- insufficient literacy skills

- lack of confidence

- language barriers

- transport problems

At level 4 you could give an example of a situation with a student for each of the needs you have listed, stating why it might occur. For example, a student might have insufficient literacy skills because it was not identified through initial assessment. The situation therefore did not come to your attention until the student submitted their first assignment.

Q12 Describe (level 3) or review (level 4) points of referral to meet these needs.

Your response could describe how the potential needs of students you have listed in Q11 can be addressed.

For example, if a student has transport problems you could find out why this was before referring them elsewhere. It could be that the bus times are not suitable for the student to arrive on time and you are aware of a different bus they could take. If this was not the case, you could advise them to ask if any other students are able to give them a lift. However, this might not be appropriate in certain situations. Alternatively, you could advise your student to find out whether any different transport is available, along with the times and costs. This would be by directing them to an appropriate company or website, not by doing it for them. If your student is unable to attend some sessions, or is late due to transport problems then this will impact upon their learning.

You could make a list of the names of people, agencies, organisations, websites, etc. who you could refer your student to when a situation arises. If you are currently teaching, you could find out if this information is already available and compare it to your own list.

Examples could include:

- names of staff within your organisation with telephone extension numbers

- external agencies such as abuse, alcohol, bereavement support, debt, drug, Samaritans, etc. along with telephone numbers or website addresses

- addresses and telephone numbers of health centres, transport companies, financial institutions, government agencies, etc.

At level 4 you will need to review the points of referral, for example, how effective a certain agency might be and what they can do to help your students.

If you are currently teaching, you could produce a case study of how you have referred a particular (anonymous) student to another person or agency, how effective this was, what the outcome was, along with the impact upon the student.

> Level 3 – 2.3 Summarise own responsibilities in relation to other professionals
>
> Level 4 – 2.3 Evaluate own responsibilities in relation to other professionals

Q13 What are your responsibilities in relation to other professionals?

Your response could break down your responsibilities into individual, team and organisational. For example, an individual responsibility towards other teachers would be to leave the teaching environment in a clean, tidy and secure manner. A team responsibility would be to work together, perhaps creating resources which could be shared. An organisational responsibility would be to ensure your administrative work was up to date, for example, records such as the register. This should all be carried out and communicated in a professional manner.

At level 4, you could give examples of other professionals internal to the organisation such as administration staff, caretakers, librarians, receptionists, support workers and technicians. You could state what your responsibility is to them, for example, if you need a handout photocopying by the administrative staff you might need to submit it by a certain time and justify why you need it. Some organisations might encourage electronic handouts rather than hard copies due to environmental or sustainability policies. You could also elaborate upon your role with other professionals external to your organisation, for example, employers, inspectors, parents, guardians and visitors.

You could elaborate on how you should represent yourself in a professional manner when dealing with other professionals. No matter what personal opinions or issues you might have, these should not impede upon your professional role.

Q14 Summarise (level 3) or evaluate (level 4) these responsibilities.

Your response could summarise each of the responsibilities you identified for the individual, team and organisation. For example, the responsibility of completing the register is to comply with the organisational requirement of documenting who is in the building at a given time. A register can be used for statistical purposes, for example, to track who attended and when. It is an auditable document and can be used for financial reasons if funding is being claimed, or if students receive a payment for attending, for example, through an apprenticeship programme.

At level 4 you could evaluate your responsibilities further, for example, stating what would happen if you forgot to complete the register. You could compare the differences between manual and electronic registration systems, or teacher versus student-led systems. You could also obtain a copy of the relevant attendance policy if you are currently teaching and evaluate its requirements.

Theory focus

References and further information

Francis, M and Gould, J (2009) *Achieving your PTLLS Award*. London: Sage Publications Ltd.

Gravells, A (2012) *Preparing to Teach in the Lifelong Learning Sector: The New Award* (5th Edn). London: Learning Matters.

IfL (2008) *Code of Professional Practice*. London: Institute for Learning.

Reece, I and Walker, S (2007) *Teaching, Training and Learning: A Practical Guide* (6th Edn). Tyne & Wear: Business Education Publishers.

Tummons, J (2010) *Becoming a Professional Tutor in the Lifelong Learning Sector* (2nd Edn). Exeter: Learning Matters.

Wallace, S (2011) *Teaching, Tutoring and Training in the Lifelong Learning Sector* (4th Edn). Exeter: Learning Matters.

Williams, J (2012) *Study Skills for PTLLS* (2nd Edn). London: Learning Matters.

Wilson, L (2008) *Practical Teaching: A Guide to PTLLS and CTLLS*. London: Cengage Learning.

Websites

Brainboxx (teachers and professionalism) – http://www.brainboxx.co.uk/a3_aspects/pages/professional.htm

Institute for Learning – www.ifl.ac.uk

Learning and Skills Improvement Service – www.lsis.org.uk

Post Compulsory Education & Training Network – www.pcet.net

UNIT TITLE: Roles, responsibilities and relationships in lifelong learning
LEVEL 3

Learning Outcomes	Assessment Criteria		Example evidence
The learner will:	The learner can:		
2. Understand the relationships between teachers and other professionals in lifelong learning	2.1	Explain the boundaries between the teaching role and other professional roles	A list of boundaries that a teacher might encounter. An explanation of what these boundaries are and how they relate to the teaching role and other professionals.
	2.2	Describe points of referral to meet the needs of learners	A list of potential needs of students. A description of relevant points of referral and support systems available such as people, agencies, organisations, websites, etc.
	2.3	Summarise own responsibilities in relation to other professionals	A list of teaching responsibilities. A summary of these responsibilities in relation to other professionals.

UNIT TITLE: Roles, responsibilities and relationships in lifelong learning
LEVEL 4

Learning Outcomes The learner will:	Assessment Criteria The learner can:		Example evidence
2. Understand the relationships between teachers and other professionals in lifelong learning	2.1	Analyse the boundaries between the teaching role and other professional roles	A list of boundaries that a teacher might encounter. An analysis of what these boundaries are and how they relate to the teaching role and other professionals.
	2.2	Review points of referral to meet the needs of learners	A list of potential needs of students. A review of the potential needs of students along with relevant points of referral and support systems available such as people, agencies, organisations, websites, etc. A case study of how a student's needs were ascertained and met.
	2.3	Evaluate own responsibilities in relation to other professionals	A list of teaching responsibilities. An evaluation of these responsibilities, with specific examples of relationships with other professionals.

CHAPTER 3
UNDERSTAND OWN RESPONSIBILITY FOR MAINTAINING A SAFE AND SUPPORTIVE LEARNING ENVIRONMENT

This chapter is in two parts. The first part: **Self assessment activities**, contains questions and activities which relate to the third learning outcome of the PTLLS unit **Roles, responsibilities and relationships in lifelong learning**.

The assessment criteria for each level are shown in boxes and are followed by questions and activities for you to carry out. Ensure your responses are *specific to you*, the *subject* you will teach and the *context* and *environment* in which you will teach.

After completing the activities and questions, check your responses with the second part: **Guidance for evidencing achievement**. This guidance is not intended to give you the answers to questions you may be asked in any formal assessments; however, it will help you focus your responses towards meeting the PTLLS assessment criteria.

At the end of each chapter is an example of a completed assessment grid at level 3 and level 4. These give examples of evidence you could provide towards the assessment criteria. Evidence can be cross-referenced between units and assessment criteria if it meets the requirements.

Self assessment activities

Level 3 – 3.1 Explain own responsibilities in maintaining a safe and supportive learning environment

Level 4 – 3.1 Explain how to establish and maintain a safe and supportive learning environment

Q15 What do you consider a safe and supportive learning environment to be?

Q16 Explain your responsibilities in maintaining a safe and supportive learning environment.

Level 3 – 3.2 Explain ways to promote appropriate behaviour and respect for others

Level 4 – 3.2 Explain how to promote appropriate behaviour and respect for others

Q17 What do you consider is appropriate behaviour and respect for others?

Q18 How can you promote appropriate behaviour and respect for others?

Guidance for evidencing achievement

Level 3 – 3.1 Explain own responsibilities in maintaining a safe and support-ive learning environment

Level 4 – 3.1 Explain how to establish and maintain a safe and supportive learning environment

Q15 What do you consider a safe and supportive learning environment to be?

Your response could state that all aspects of the learning environment i.e. *physical*, *social* and *learning* should be appropriate, accessible and safe for the subject you will teach. Informing your students how you and the organisation will ensure their safety towards each aspect would help make them feel more comfortable. Students need to know they are safe when they are with you and not in any danger. For example, resources should not cause harm, desks should be in an appropriate layout, heating, lighting and ventilation should be adequate (physical). Safe also relates to students feeling safe to express their opinions without being ridiculed. Students should also know that you, their peers and others if necessary, will make their time in the learning environment supportive and productive (social). Supportive also relates to giving appropriate advice and/or referring your students to others if you can't help them with something. Your session should have a clear aim and convey how your students will be supported towards achievement (learning). You should also demonstrate inclusion and challenge any inappropriate or anti-social behaviour. Ensuring your students can have a break (if applicable), and have access to refreshment areas and toilets will help them feel comfortable in the learning environment.

At level 4 you could relate your response to quotes from text books. For example, ... *learners need to feel safe and valued before they can fulfil their potential for learning* (Wallace, 2011: 96). You could then explain what you consider a safe environment to be, and how you will help students fulfil their potential to learn. If you are currently teaching, you could find out what the policies are at your organisation and explain how these will ensure your students are safe and supported.

Q16 Explain your responsibilities in maintaining a safe and supportive learning environment.

Your response could explain how the physical, social and learning aspects can impact upon each other, giving examples. If the room you are in is too cold, students might not be able to concentrate, how could you overcome this? If desks are in rows, students might not be able to communicate well, could you safely rearrange the tables to alleviate this? If you are currently teaching, you should have a job description which will outline your responsibilities. Whilst it is your responsibility to ensure the environment is safe and supportive, you might not be able to control some aspects such as lighting, ventilation, etc. However, what you can do is ensure your session is interesting, meaningful and engaging to your students. You would need to take into account your organisation's Health and Safety policy and not do anything outside of your own responsibility, such as moving heavy equipment or asking your students to work with hazardous materials. Some resources, particularly electrical ones, require regular maintenance checks and testing. If you see a label on a resource which shows it hasn't been checked for a long time, you will need to liaise with the relevant personnel to ensure it is checked.

Creating a supportive learning environment will include agreeing ground rules, planning your sessions to be inclusive, motivating your students, encouraging your students to become actively involved and giving regular feedback. You could also encourage peer support though the *buddy* approach. This enables students to pair up with someone in the group they feel comfortable with, they can then keep in touch with them outside of your sessions.

Your responsibilities might include undertaking a Criminal Records Bureau (CRB) check to confirm you do not have a criminal record, although your organisation might arrange this. You might also have to attend relevant training such as Safeguarding, and Equality and Diversity. If you are registered with the Institute for Learning (IfL) you will need to abide by their Code of Professional Practice (2008), which has *reasonable care* as one of the seven teaching behaviours.

Keeping records such as a register will prove useful should there be a need to evacuate the building. You should also be aware of the accident, fire and emergency procedures within your organisation. The Health and Safety at Work etc Act (1974) makes it your responsibility to report a hazard if you see it. There are many issues you might come across where you will need to liaise with others, you could therefore create a list of helpful people you could contact, with their details.

At level 4 you could explain how you would *establish and maintain* a safe and supportive learning environment. Establishing a safe environment can include checking the environment you will be in, and carrying out any necessary risk assessments. You might notice some resources are not working and will therefore need to report them to be fixed, or a window that is stuck in a closed position but will need to be opened to let in fresh air. Maintaining a safe environment involves being aware of any potential issues and dealing with them as soon as possible. You could also research and explain the *reasonable care* behaviour of the IfL Code of Professional Practice (2008).

Establishing a supportive environment can include identifying any particular student needs or concerns to help you address them. Initial and diagnostic assessments could be used before students commence to ascertain this information. Using appropriate and varied teaching approaches can help include all students, for example, by using a variety of activities to address all learning styles.

You could cross-reference your response to Q2, Q7 and Q8 in Chapter 1 (assessment criteria 1.1 and 1.4) regarding Health and Safety, student needs, Maslow's Hierarchy of Needs (1962), Fleming's (2005) and Honey and Mumford's (1992) learning styles if you mentioned these previously.

If you are currently teaching, you could produce a case study of how you have established and maintained a safe and supportive learning environment for your students.

> Level 3 – 3.2 Explain ways to promote appropriate behaviour and respect for others
>
> Level 4 – 3.2 Explain how to promote appropriate behaviour and respect for others

Q17 What do you consider is appropriate behaviour and respect for others?

You could start by explaining that you would *lead by example* and model good practice. If you demonstrate appropriate behaviour and respect for others, hopefully your students and others will emulate this. Being a professional involves acting with integrity, behaving in the correct manner for your role, and respecting others as you would wish them to respect you. You should follow relevant Codes of Practice, for example, the IfL Code of Professional Practice (2008) which includes behaviour and respect.

Appropriate behaviour includes:

- adhering to relevant policies and procedures
- arriving early to ensure the environment is appropriate
- agreeing ground rules with students
- being honest, reliable and trustworthy
- challenging and managing inappropriate behaviour of others
- ensuring the learning environment is safe and suitable
- establishing routines
- liaising and working with others in a professional manner
- maintaining up to date records
- not overstepping the boundaries of your role
- preparing adequately for your sessions
- reporting concerns
- returning marked work within agreed timescales
- remaining impartial in any disputes
- supporting your students as necessary
- using a variety of inclusive teaching and learning approaches

Respect includes valuing others' opinions and not imposing your own upon them.

At level 4 you could use quotes from text books in your response, and then relate them to how you will behave with your own students. For example, *A good first impression will help establish a positive working relationship with your students. The way you dress, act, respond to questions, offer support etc, will also influence your students* (Gravells, 2012: 10). *The teacher can themselves provide a model of appropriate behaviour* (Wallace, 2007: 79). You could then state that by being early to sessions, following the ground rules, treating all students as individuals and teaching in an inclusive way, you will hopefully help students emulate your positive behaviour.

Q18 How can you promote appropriate behaviour and respect for others?

Your response could explain the way you would put into practice each of the statements you gave in answer to Q17. For *challenging and managing inappropriate behaviour of others* you could describe what you would do in a certain situation, for example, if a colleague did something you believe to be unacceptable. You could have a quiet word with them, or if it is serious you might need to report them to someone else. If you are currently teaching, you could link your response to your organisation's policies and procedures.

At level 4 you need to explain how you would promote appropriate behaviour and respect for others. This is not just your own behaviour, but that of others, for example, your students. You could use a quote from a text book, state whether you agree or disagree with it and why, and then explain what you would do.

Theory focus

References and further information

Fleming, N (2005) *Teaching and Learning Styles: VARK Strategies*. Honolulu: Honolulu Community College.

Gravells, A (2012) *Preparing to Teach in the Lifelong Learning Sector: The New Award* (5th Edn). London: Learning Matters.

IfL (2008) *Code of Professional Practice*. London: Institute for Learning.

Reece, I and Walker, S (2007) *Teaching, Training and Learning: A Practical Guide* (6th Edn). Tyne & Wear: Business Education Publishers.

Tummons, J (2010) *Becoming a Professional Tutor in the Lifelong Learning Sector* (2nd Edn). Exeter: Learning Matters.

Tummons, J (2011) *Assessing Learning in the Lifelong Learning Sector* (3rd Edn). Exeter: Learning Matters.

Vizard, D (2007) *How to Manage Behaviour in Further Education*. London: Sage Publications Ltd.

Wallace, S (2007) *Managing Behaviour in the Lifelong Learning Sector*. Exeter: Learning Matters.

Wallace, S (2011) *Teaching, Tutoring and Training in the Lifelong Learning Sector* (4th Edn). Exeter: Learning Matters.

Websites

Criminal Records Bureau (CRB) – www.crb.gov.uk

Data Protection Act (2003) – http://regulatorylaw.co.uk/Data_Protection_Act_2003.html

Equality & Diversity Forum – www.edf.org.uk

Fleming's Learning Styles – www.vark-learn.com

Health & Safety at Work etc Act (1974) – http://www.hse.gov.uk/legislation/hswa.htm

Institute for Learning – www.ifl.ac.uk

Risk assessments – http://www.hse.gov.uk/risk/fivesteps.htm

Safeguarding Vulnerable Groups Act (2006) – http://www.opsi.gov.uk/ACTS/acts2006/ukpga_20060047_en_1

UNIT TITLE: Roles, responsibilities and relationships in lifelong learning

LEVEL 3

Learning Outcomes The learner will:	Assessment Criteria The learner can:	Example evidence
3. Understand own responsibility for maintaining a safe and supportive learning environment	3.1 Explain own responsibilities in maintaining a safe and supportive learning environment	An explanation of own responsibilities towards maintaining a safe and supportive learning environment. Job description. Relevant organisation policies and procedures. A list of helpful contacts. CRB certificate. Evidence of complying with legal/regulatory requirements. Records of risk assessments. Records of training attended such as Health & Safety and Safeguarding. *Cross-referenced to Roles, responsibilities and relationships in lifelong learning 1.1 and 1.4.*
	3.2 Explain ways to promote appropriate behaviour and respect for others	An explanation of ways to promote appropriate behaviour and respect for others.

UNIT TITLE: Roles, responsibilities and relationships in lifelong learning

LEVEL 4

Learning Outcomes The learner will:	Assessment Criteria The learner can:		Example evidence
3. Understand own responsibility for maintaining a safe and supportive learning environment	3.1	Explain how to establish and maintain a safe and supportive learning environment	An explanation of own responsibilities towards maintaining a safe and supportive learning environment. Job description. Relevant organisation policies and procedures. A list of helpful contacts. CRB certificate. Evidence of complying with legal/regulatory requirements. Records of risk assessments. Records of training attended such as Health & Safety and Safeguarding. A case study of how you have established and maintained a safe and supportive learning environment. *Cross-referenced to Roles, responsibilities and relationships in lifelong learning 1.1 and 1.4.*
	3.2	Explain how to promote appropriate behaviour and respect for others	An explanation of how to promote appropriate behaviour and respect for others. Examples of putting these into practice with links to policies and procedures.

This chapter is in two parts. The first part: *Self assessment activities*, contains questions and activities which relate to the first learning outcome of the PTLLS unit *Understanding inclusive learning and teaching in lifelong learning*.

The assessment criteria for each level are shown in boxes and are followed by questions and activities for you to carry out. Ensure your responses are *specific to you*, the *subject* you will teach and the *context* and *environment* in which you will teach.

After completing the activities, check your responses with the second part: *Guidance for evidencing achievement*. This guidance is not intended to give you the answers to questions you may be asked in any formal assessments; however, it will help you focus your responses towards meeting the PTLLS assessment criteria.

At the end of each chapter is an example of a completed assessment grid at level 3 and level 4. These give examples of evidence you could provide towards the assessment criteria. Evidence can be cross-referenced between units and assessment criteria if it meets the requirements.

Self assessment activities

Level 3 – 1.1 Summarise learning and teaching strategies used in own specialism

Level 4 – 1.1 Analyse learning and teaching strategies used in own specialism

Q19 **What learning and teaching strategies could you use for your specialist subject?**

Q20 **Summarise (level 3) or analyse (level 4) these strategies.**

> Level 3 – 1.2 Explain how approaches to learning and teaching in own specialism meet the needs of learners
>
> Level 4 – 1.2 Evaluate the effectiveness of approaches to learning and teaching in own specialist area in meeting needs of learners

Q21 Explain (level 3) or evaluate (level 4) the effectiveness of learning and teaching approaches in meeting the needs of students.

> Level 3 – 1.3 Describe aspects of inclusive learning
>
> Level 4 – 1.3 Evaluate aspects of inclusive learning

Q22 What does inclusive learning mean?

Q23 Describe (level 3) or evaluate (level 4) ways of incorporating inclusive learning during your sessions.

Guidance for evidencing achievement

Level 3 – 1.1 Summarise learning and teaching strategies used in own specialism

Level 4 – 1.1 Analyse learning and teaching strategies used in own specialism

Q19 What learning and teaching strategies could you use for your specialist subject?

Your response could include strategies such as:

- demonstrations
- discussions
- distance and/or online learning
- e-learning
- group work
- individual work
- project work
- presentations
- research
- role plays
- seminars
- simulations
- use of information and communication technology (ICT)

The strategies will very much depend upon the *subject* you are teaching, and the *context* and *environment* you are teaching in. However, you should choose strategies which will engage, stimulate and motivate your students to achieve their full potential.

Q20 Summarise (level 3) or analyse (level 4) these strategies.

Your response could summarise the strengths and limitations of each strategy, perhaps in a table, for example,

Strategy	Strengths	Limitations
Demonstrations	A practical way of showing how something works. Allows time for questions and for students to have a go themselves. Links theory and practice. A handout can be given to supplement the demonstration. Can cover all learning styles.	Resources might not be available. Takes time to prepare. Not all students might be able to see if they in a large group. Individuals might not pay attention.
Discussions	All students can be encouraged to participate. Useful to assess knowledge and understanding.	Some students might not wish to be involved. The group needs to remain focused as it can be easy to digress.

At level 4 you could analyse the strategies by giving an example of how you would use each of them with your students. If you demonstrated a subject to a group of 15 students, you could explain how you prepared for the demonstration, what resources you used and why, how you involved all your students and how effective the demonstration process was.

You could relate your response to quotes from text books, for example, *Demonstration – explains difficult parts of the task when verbal exposition is not suitable* (Wilson, 2008: 35). You could then state what you would do differently and why.

> Level 3 – 1.2 Explain how approaches to learning and teaching in own specialism meet the needs of learners
>
> Level 4 – 1.2 Evaluate the effectiveness of approaches to learning and teaching in own specialist area in meeting needs of learners

Q21 Explain (level 3) or evaluate (level 4) the effectiveness of learning and teaching approaches in meeting the needs of students.

Your response could explain the approaches you will use for the different teaching strategies listed in your response to Q19, and how effective they will be. Your main approach might be a mixture of discussion, group work and questions in a workshop or training room. Alternatively, you might use a blended approach of teaching in a classroom with support and activities via a virtual learning environment (VLE). You might set tasks which differentiate for your students in each of these, which stretch and challenge higher level students, or enable slower students to catch up.

You might use a demonstration for a practical task as it is a way of incorporating all learning styles. Students can watch the demonstration (visual), listen to an explanation (aural), read instructions on a handout and make notes (read/write), and then practise the task (kinaesthetic). You could explain how effective this type of approach is in meeting the needs of individual and multi-modal learning styles.

Whether you are teaching individuals or groups will determine the approaches you take. You could explain the different strategies you would use to enable learning to take place, such as coaching, instruction, lectures, group work, etc., stating how adaptable they would be in different situations and with different students. You could also explain how varying your approaches during a session can help retain student attention. Different approaches can help ascertain any particular student needs and lead to opportunities for additional support such as literacy and numeracy.

You could also explain your own personal approach to teaching, such as passion for your subject and the enthusiastic way in which you will deliver it.

At level 4 you could evaluate the effectiveness of your approaches to meet the needs of your students. If you use activities which meet all the learning styles you could compare and contrast theorists such as Fleming's (1987) VARK, Honey and Mumford's (1986) activist, pragmatist, theorist and reflector and Laird's (1985) sensory theory of sight, hearing, touch, smell and taste (as in Gravells, 2012).

You could mention Knowles (1978), who is the theorist who brought the concept of adult learning to the fore. He argued that adulthood takes place when people behave in adult ways and believe themselves to be adults. Most formal education still focuses on the teacher as the provider of knowledge (pedagogy) rather than the student being at the centre of the learning process (andragogy). Using an andragogical approach encourages active learning rather than passive learning, with you as the teacher acting as a facilitator. However, the approach you take will very much depend upon the subject you are teaching. Taking a pedagogical approach will not suit all students and may make them switch off from the learning process. You might also consider which *domain* you want to reach, for example,

Bloom's (1956) cognitive, affective and psycho motor domains. Think of cognitive as the *head*, i.e. knowledge, affective as the *heart*, i.e. feelings, and psycho motor as the hands, i.e. *skills*. These will also affect the approaches you decide to use.

> Level 3 – 1.3 Describe aspects of inclusive learning
>
> Level 4 – 1.3 Evaluate aspects of inclusive learning

Q22 What does inclusive learning mean?

Your response could state that inclusive learning is about involving all your students during the session, treating them equally and fairly and not directly or indirectly excluding anyone for any reason. You should also take into account any individual learning or support needs.

At level 4 you could compare and contrast different meanings of inclusion such as Wilson (2008: 296) who states *inclusion simply means 'available to all'*. Tummons (2010: 93) states *inclusive practice can be defined as an approach to teaching and learning that endeavours to encourage the fullest participation of learners*. After comparing and contrasting the quotes you could state how you would apply them in practice.

Q23 Describe (level 3) or evaluate (level 4) ways of incorporating inclusive learning during your sessions.

Your response will depend upon whether you teach individuals or groups. With individuals, you will be able to dedicate your time to their needs and help them achieve their potential. With groups, you will need to be aware of aspects such as attention spans, learning styles and any individual needs. Using eye contact with all students, asking open questions to everyone at some point during the session and using names are ways to make each student feel included by the teacher.

Using a mixture of different approaches within your sessions will ensure you meet all learning styles and retain student engagement and motivation. If you plan to use group activities consider which students will work together in case students with strong personalities dominate and change the group dynamics. Equally, make sure any quiet students are able to participate and be involved. If you use a student-centred rather than a teacher-centred approach you will need to be confident in the way you manage the activities. For example, if students are researching then presenting a topic, you will need to ensure they are capable of working together.

You will need to be aware of any challenges to inclusive learning such as a lack of confidence or a fear of embarrassment in front of their peers. There may also be barriers such as an inappropriate room layout which does not encourage group work.

At level 4 you could evaluate ways of incorporating inclusive learning during your sessions. You could produce a case study (hypothetical or real) of how you ensured all your students were included during a particular session, evaluating how this happened and what the possible consequences of not including everyone could be. You could also relate your response to quotes from text books, for example, *If we are to be effective in our teaching, all learners should feel part of and engaged in the particular session. If this is the case, our approach would be said to be demonstrating inclusion* (Francis and Gould, 2009: 73).

Theory focus

References and further information

Bloom, BS (1956) *Taxonomy of Educational Objectives: Handbook 1*. New York: Longman.

Francis, M and Gould, J (2009) *Achieving your PTLLS Award*. London: Sage Publications Ltd.

Gravells, A (2012) *Preparing to Teach in the Lifelong Learning Sector: The New Award* (5th Edn). London: Learning Matters.

Knowles, MS, Holton, EF and Swanson, RA (2005) *The Adult Learner: The definitive classic in adult education and human resource development*. Oxford: Butterworth-Heinemann.

Reece, I and Walker, S (2007) *Teaching, Training and Learning: A Practical Guide* (6th Edn). Tyne & Wear: Business Education Publishers.

Tummons, J (2010) *Becoming a Professional Tutor in the Lifelong Learning Sector* (2nd Edn). Exeter: Learning Matters.

Wallace, S (2011) *Teaching, Tutoring and Training in the Lifelong Learning Sector* (4th Edn). Exeter: Learning Matters.

Wilson, L (2008) *Practical Teaching: A Guide to PTLLS and CTLLS*. London: Cengage Learning.

Websites

Approaches to teaching and learning – http://www.excellencegateway.org.uk/page.aspx?o=127654

Inclusive teaching – http://www.open.ac.uk/inclusiveteaching/pages/inclusive-teaching/index.php

UNIT TITLE: Understanding inclusive learning and teaching in lifelong learning

LEVEL 3 (3 credits)

Learning Outcomes The learner will:	Assessment Criteria The learner can:		Example evidence
1. Understand learning and teaching strategies in lifelong learning	1.1	Summarise learning and teaching strategies used in own specialism	A summary of relevant learning and teaching strategies which relate to your specialist subject. A list of the strengths and limitations of each strategy. Scheme of work, session plan or individual learning plan showing strategies to be used.
	1.2	Explain how approaches to learning and teaching in own specialism meet the needs of learners	An explanation of how approaches to learning and teaching in your specialist subject can meet the needs of students, with examples.
	1.3	Describe aspects of inclusive learning	A description of inclusive learning. An explanation of how you can include students during a session.

UNIT TITLE: Understanding inclusive learning and teaching in lifelong learning

LEVEL 4 (3 credits)

Learning Outcomes	Assessment Criteria		Example evidence
The learner will:	The learner can:		
1. Understand learning and teaching strategies in lifelong learning	1.1	Analyse learning and teaching strategies used in own specialism	An analysis of specific examples of relevant learning and teaching strategies which relate to your specialist subject. A list of the strengths and limitations of each strategy. Scheme of work, session plan or individual learning plan showing strategies to be used. Evidence of adapting and using various approaches and resources. A comparison of relevant strategies and theories.
	1.2	Evaluate the effectiveness of approaches to learning and teaching in own specialist area in meeting needs of learners	An evaluation of how approaches to learning and teaching in your specialist subject can meet the needs of students. An evaluation of specific examples stating what you would change and why to meet particular student needs.
	1.3	Evaluate aspects of inclusive learning	A description of inclusive learning. An evaluation of how you can include students during a particular session. A case study regarding inclusive learning.

CHAPTER 5
UNDERSTAND HOW TO CREATE INCLUSIVE LEARNING AND TEACHING IN LIFELONG LEARNING

This chapter is in two parts. The first part: **Self assessment activities**, contains questions and activities which relate to the second learning outcome of the PTLLS unit **Understanding inclusive learning and teaching in lifelong learning**.

The assessment criteria for each level are shown in boxes and are followed by questions and activities for you to carry out. Ensure your responses are specific to you, the subject you will teach and the context and environment in which you will teach.

After completing the activities, check your responses with the second part: **Guidance for evidencing achievement**. This guidance is not intended to give you the answers to questions you may be asked in any formal assessments; however, it will help you focus your responses towards meeting the PTLLS assessment criteria.

At the end of each chapter is an example of a completed assessment grid at level 3 and level 4. These give examples of evidence you could provide towards the assessment criteria. Evidence can be cross-referenced between units and assessment criteria if it meets the requirements.

Self assessment activities

Level 3 – 2.1 Explain how to select inclusive learning and teaching techniques

Level 4 – 2.1 Analyse inclusive approaches to learning and teaching

Q24 Explain (level 3) or analyse (level 4) how you would decide which inclusive learning and teaching techniques you could use.

Level 3 – 2.2 Explain how to select resources that meet the needs of learners

Level 4 – 2.2 Analyse how to select resources to meet the needs of learners

Q25 Explain (level 3) or analyse (level 4) how to select resources that will meet the needs of your students.

> Level 3 – 2.3 Explain how to create assessment opportunities that meet the needs of learners
>
> Level 4 – 2.3 Explain how to create assessment opportunities that meet the needs of learners

Q26 Explain how you could create assessment opportunities that meet the needs of your students.

> Level 3 – 2.4 Explain how to provide opportunities for learners to practise their literacy, language, numeracy and ICT skills
>
> Level 4 – 2.4 Review how to provide opportunities for learners to practise their literacy, language, numeracy and ICT skills

Q27 Explain (level 3) or review (level 4) how you could provide opportunities for your students to practise their literacy, language, numeracy and ICT skills.

Guidance for evidencing achievement

Level 3 – 2.1 Explain how to select inclusive learning and teaching techniques

Level 4 – 2.1 Analyse inclusive approaches to learning and teaching

Q24 Explain (level 3) or analyse (level 4) how you would decide which inclusive learning and teaching techniques you could use.

Your response could explain that the techniques you use will be based upon the requirements of the subject you will teach. This will involve obtaining and reading the syllabus or qualification handbook from the awarding organisation if the programme you are teaching is accredited. If it is non-accredited, i.e. does not lead to a recognised certificate, your techniques might be based upon your organisation's recommendations. Your own skills and knowledge might influence the techniques you use, for example, you might ask visiting speakers to talk to your students, or you could arrange visits to appropriate locations. Other factors include the environment within which you will teach as this could affect the techniques you decide to use. This could be a classroom, workshop, training room, outdoor environment, etc. You will need to explain the techniques you would use in your particular environment and context, for example, a prison, college or the workplace. You might also be influenced by what resources and equipment are available and whether you teach individuals or groups. The time of day could also have an affect, for example, you might wish to use an energiser activity after a lunch break in case your learners feel tired. All the techniques you use should be inclusive to your students, and not exclude anyone for any reason. You could cross-reference your response to Q19 and Q23 in Chapter 4 (assessment criteria 1.1 and 1.3).

At level 4 you could analyse the techniques you will use based upon the requirements of your subject. If you tend to use a lot of group work you could relate your response to theorists such as Tuckman's (1965 and 1975) group formation theory of forming, storming, norming, performing and adjourning. You could compare and contrast this to Belbin's (1993) team roles. If you mainly teach individuals you could explore Berne's (1964) Transactional Analysis theory regarding the roles individuals take on in different situations. These theories can be found in Gravells (2012). Being aware of these theories will help you understand why your students act differently and what happens in certain situations.

> Level 3 – 2.2 Explain how to select resources that meet the needs of learners
>
> Level 4 – 2.2 Analyse how to select resources to meet the needs of learners

Q25 Explain (level 3) or analyse (level 4) how to select resources that will meet the needs of your students.

Your response will depend upon the *subject and level* and the *context and environment* within which you will teach. You could explain what resources you would select depending upon what you wish to achieve, for example, a handout to promote understanding, a physical resource to arouse interest, computer access to provide variety, etc. Resources should always be based upon the needs of your students. There's no point using a particular resource just because you enjoy using it; your students must be able to benefit from it.

Some examples of resources are:

- audio/visual/digital equipment

- computerised presentations

- computers and multi media

- flip chart paper and pens

- handouts

- interactive whiteboards

- overhead projector

- physical resources, models and apparatus

- text books

- worksheets, puzzles and crosswords

You could then explain the strengths and limitations of each for your particular subject and students.

If you teach a practical subject you might use specialist equipment and will need to ensure it has been properly serviced or tested and meets any health and safety requirements. All resources used should be appropriate in terms of quality, quantity and content and be relevant to the subject, level and the learning expected.

At level 4 you will need to analyse how you would select certain resources, for example, you might select a handout which incorporates an activity. However, based upon feedback from previous students you might decide to amend it in some way. You could also relate your response to quotes from relevant text books, for example, *Resources should be: 1 simple, 2 to the point, 3 interesting* (Reece and Walker, 2007: 158). You could state how you would ensure you meet these requirements with the resources you would use.

If you are currently teaching, you could produce a case study regarding a resource you have used, how effective it was, how learning took place and how it met the needs of your students.

> Level 3 – 2.3 Explain how to create assessment opportunities that meet the needs of learners
>
> Level 4 – 2.3 Explain how to create assessment opportunities that meet the needs of learners

Q26 Explain how you could create assessment opportunities that meet the needs of your students.

Your response could state that during a session, assessment can be initial (at the beginning), formative (during) and summative (at the end). To create an assessment opportunity at the beginning of a session you could ask your students if anyone has any knowledge of the topic. This would enable you to include their experiences and promote discussions. Opportunities for formative assessment can occur throughout the session by asking questions and observing actions. Opportunities for summative assessment could occur through an assignment or test. The assessment activities must meet the needs of your students, for example, asking oral questions rather than issuing written questions if necessary. They should also be applicable to individuals or groups and meet the requirements of the subject.

At level 4 you could produce a case study of an assessment activity you could use, explaining how the opportunities would arise to use it, and how it would meet the needs of particular students.

If you are working towards the unit *Principles of assessment in lifelong learning* you could cross-reference this response to Q41, Q42 and Q43 in Chapter 10 (assessment criteria 1.1, 1.2 and 1.3).

> Level 3 – 2.4 Explain how to provide opportunities for learners to practise their literacy, language, numeracy and ICT skills
>
> Level 4 – 2.4 Review how to provide opportunities for learners to practise their literacy, language, numeracy and ICT skills

Q27 Explain (level 3) or review (level 4) how you could provide opportunities for your students to practise their literacy, language, numeracy and ICT skills.

Your response could explain how you can provide opportunities for your students to practise their literacy, language, numeracy and ICT skills within your sessions.

Examples include:

- Literacy – reading and writing

- Language – listening, speaking and discussing

- Numeracy – approximations, estimations, calculations and measurements

- ICT – use of e-mail, web-based research, word processing of assignments and reports, using spreadsheets, databases and presentation packages

To explain how you will do this you will need to give specific examples which relate to your specialist subject. An example for cookery would be:

- Literacy – reading recipes, making notes and writing a list of ingredients

- Language – discussing recipes, debating where to purchase ingredients, listening and asking questions, talking to others, presenting ideas

- Numeracy – calculating weights, calculating the costs of ingredients, measuring amounts, estimating calorific values, cooking times and temperatures

- ICT – using a word processor to produce a menu, researching recipes and healthy eating websites, accessing forums, e-mailing other students

At level 4 you could review how you can provide opportunities for your students to practise their literacy, language, numeracy and ICT skills within your sessions. You could relate your response to quotes from text books, for example, *When teaching, it's best to find naturally occurring opportunities whenever possible as this will enable your students to see it as part of the subject, not a separate session* (Gravells, 2012: 79). You could then review how you could use naturally occurring opportunities.

If you are currently teaching, you could produce a case study, experimenting with different opportunities and activities for literacy, language, numeracy and ICT. You could then evaluate them by assessing their success or otherwise. Asking your students how they felt their skills have improved as a result will give you valuable feedback, enabling you to take a different approach next time if necessary.

Theory focus

References and further information

Belbin, M (1993) *Team Roles At Work*. Oxford: Elsevier Science & Technology.

Berne, E (1964) Games People Play – The Psychology of Human Relationships. London: Penguin Books.

Bloom, BS (Ed) (1956) *The Taxonomy of Educational Objectives, The Classification of Educational Goals*. New York: McKay.

Gravells, A (2008) *PTLLS: The New Award*. London: Learning Matters.

Gravells, A and Simpson, S (2012) *Equality and Diversity in the Lifelong Learning Sector* (2nd Edn). London: Learning Matters.

Knowles, MS (1978) *The Adult Learner; A Neglected Species* (2nd Edn). Gulf Publishing.

Reece, I and Walker, S (2007) *Teaching, Training and Learning: A Practical Guide* (6th Edn). Tyne & Wear: Business Education Publishers.

Skills for Business (2007) *Inclusive learning approaches for literacy, language, numeracy and ICT*. London: LLUK.

Websites

Fleming's learning styles – www.vark-learn.com

Honey and Mumford learning styles – www.peterhoney.com

Teaching resources, support and advice – http://www.excellencegateway.org.uk/page.aspx?o=home

Theories of learning – www.learningandteaching.info/learning/

Tuckman – www.infed.org/thinkers/tuckman.htm

Resources for teaching and learning – http://www.excellencegateway.org.uk/node/18239

UNIT TITLE: Understanding inclusive learning and teaching in lifelong learning
LEVEL 3 (3 credits)

Learning Outcomes The learner will:	Assessment Criteria The learner can:		Example evidence
2. Understand how to create inclusive learning and teaching in lifelong learning	2.1	Explain how to select inclusive learning and teaching techniques	An explanation of how you would select inclusive learning and teaching techniques to use with students. Syllabus or qualification handbook highlighting inclusive approaches. *Cross-referenced to the unit: Understanding inclusive learning and teaching in lifelong learning 1.1 and 1.3.*
	2.2	Explain how to select resources that meet the needs of learners	An explanation of how you have selected various resources to meet the needs of students. A list of resources with an explanation of their strengths and limitations.
	2.3	Explain how to create assessment opportunities that meet the needs of learners	An explanation of different assessment opportunities which meet the needs of students. *Cross-referenced to the unit: Principles of assessment in lifelong learning 1.1, 1.2 and 1.3.*
	2.4	Explain how to provide opportunities for learners to practise their literacy, language, numeracy and ICT skills	An explanation of how to provide opportunities for students to practise their literacy, language, numeracy and ICT skills. Examples of opportunities for activities which relate to your particular subject.

UNIT TITLE: Understanding inclusive learning and teaching in lifelong learning
LEVEL 4 (3 credits)

Learning Outcomes	Assessment Criteria		Example evidence
The learner will:	The learner can:		
2. Understand how to create inclusive learning and teaching in lifelong learning	2.1	Analyse inclusive approaches to learning and teaching	An analysis of inclusive learning and teaching approaches to use with students. Syllabus or qualification handbook highlighting inclusive approaches. A comparison of relevant teaching theories. Cross-referenced to the unit: Understanding inclusive learning and teaching in lifelong learning 1.1 and 1.3.
	2.2	Analyse how to select resources to meet the needs of learners	An analysis of how you have selected various resources to meet the needs of students. A list of resources with an analysis of their strengths and limitations. A case study regarding a resource you have used, how effective it was, how learning took place and how it met the needs of your students. Examples of resources you have used highlighting how they meet the needs of students.
	2.3	Explain how to create assessment opportunities that meet the needs of learners	An explanation of different assessment opportunities which meet the needs of students. Cross-referenced to the unit: Principles of assessment in lifelong learning 1.1, 1.2 and 1.3. A case study regarding an assessment activity used, how the opportunities arose to use it, and how it met the needs of particular students.
	2.4	Review how to provide opportunities for learners to practise their literacy, language, numeracy and ICT skills	A review of how to provide opportunities for students to practise their literacy, language, numeracy and ICT skills. Examples which relate to your particular subject. A case study evaluating different activities used with students to improve their literacy, language, numeracy and ICT skills.

CHAPTER 6
UNDERSTAND WAYS TO CREATE A MOTIVATING LEARNING ENVIRONMENT

This chapter is in two parts. The first part: *Self assessment activities*, contains questions and activities which relate to the third learning outcome of the PTLLS unit *Understanding inclusive learning and teaching in lifelong learning*.

The assessment criteria for each level are shown in boxes and are followed by questions and activities for you to carry out. Ensure your responses are *specific to you*, the *subject* you will teach and the *context* and *environment* in which you will teach.

After completing the activities, check your responses with the second part: *Guidance for evidencing achievement*. This guidance is not intended to give you the answers to questions you may be asked in any formal assessments; however, it will help you focus your responses towards meeting the PTLLS assessment criteria.

At the end of each chapter is an example of a completed assessment grid at level 3 and level 4. These give examples of evidence you could provide towards the assessment criteria. Evidence can be cross-referenced between units and assessment criteria if it meets the requirements.

Self assessment activities

Level 3 – 3.1 Explain ways to engage and motivate learners in an inclusive learning environment

Level 4 – 3.1 Explain how to engage and motivate learners in an inclusive learning environment

Q28 Explain how can you engage and motivate your students in an inclusive learning environment.

Level 3 – 3.2 Summarise ways to establish ground rules with learners to promote respect for others

Level 4 – 3.2 Explain how to establish ground rules with learners to promote respect for others

Q29 Summarise (level 3) or explain (level 4) how can you can establish ground rules with your students to promote respect for others.

Level 3 – 3.3 Explain ways to give constructive feedback that motivates learners

Level 4 – 3.3 Review ways to give constructive feedback to motivate learners

Q30 Explain (level 3) or review (level 4) how you can give constructive feedback which motivates your students.

Guidance for evidencing achievement

> Level 3 – 3.1 Explain ways to engage and motivate learners in an inclusive learning environment
>
> Level 4 – 3.1 Explain how to engage and motivate learners in an inclusive learning environment

Q28 Explain how can you engage and motivate your students in an inclusive learning environment.

Your response could explain that using varied teaching and learning approaches will help engage and motivate your students. Approaches which are active rather than passive, for example, group work, will help engage your students. Other inclusive opportunities to involve students include discussions, practical tasks and paired activities. These approaches should reach all learning styles if used well. Recognising student achievements and giving praise and encouragement can also help motivation.

You could cross-reference your response to Q23 in Chapter 4 (assessment criteria 1.3) and Q24 in Chapter 5 (assessment criteria 2.1).

At level 4 you could relate your response to quotes from relevant text books, for example, *If we are to be effective in our teaching, all learners should feel part of and engaged in the particular session* (Francis and Gould, 2009: 73). You could then state how you would engage your students for your particular subject, to ensure they are all included and motivated.

> Level 3 – 3.2 Summarise ways to establish ground rules with learners to promote respect for others
>
> Level 4 – 3.2 Explain how to establish ground rules with learners to promote respect for others

Q29 Summarise (level 3) or explain (level 4) how can you can establish ground rules with your students to promote respect for others.

Your response could state that ground rules are boundaries, rules and conditions within which students can safely work and learn. If they are followed, they should promote respect for others and ensure the sessions run smoothly.

You will need to summarise how you can establish these with your students, for example, during the first session after the icebreaker. This could be by a group activity or paired discussion. The list could be written on flip chart paper to be displayed on the wall each time the group meets to act as a visual reminder. Alternatively, a word processed version could be given to each student or uploaded to a virtual learning environment.

Ground rules should always be negotiated with your students rather than forced upon them; they will then feel included and motivated if they are involved, taking responsibility for them. Some ground rules might be re-negotiated or added to throughout the programme, for example, changing the break time. Others might not be negotiable, for example, health and safety requirements.

If ground rules are not set, problems could occur which might disrupt the session or lead to misunderstandings. Empowering students to take ownership of the ground rules should help ensure they are all followed, leading to limited disruption within the group and respect for all.

You could make a list of ground rules, for example:

- arriving on time and returning from breaks on time
- following health and safety regulations
- not eating or drinking during the session
- respecting each other's opinions
- switching off mobile phones and electronic devices

At level 4 you could explain different ways you would establish ground rules with your students. You could set and impose them, the students could set and agree them on their own, in pairs or a group, or both you and your students could work together by a process of negotiation. The best method is the latter as this enables the group to recognise what is and is not acceptable, giving them a sense of ownership and responsibility. Ground rules that are set solely by the teacher could potentially alienate the students and make them feel less respected. If a student breaks a ground rule you may find their peers reprimand them before you need to. Enabling your students to discuss and agree the ground rules allows for negotiation and understanding of the boundaries, rules and conditions in which to effectively work and learn. It also enables them to begin working together as a group and encourages aspects such as listening, compromise and respect for each other.

You could relate your response to quotes from text books, for example, *When establishing ground rules, you need to have an idea of what needs to be imposed and what could be negotiated* (Gravells, 2012: 92). You could then explain how you will decide what will be imposed and what you feel can be negotiated.

> Level 3 – 3.3 Explain ways to give constructive feedback that motivates learners
>
> Level 4 – 3.3 Review ways to give constructive feedback to motivate learners

Q30 Explain (level 3) or review (level 4) how you can give constructive feedback which motivates your students.

Your response could explain the ways you would give constructive feedback to your students. This might be informally during a session, and/or formally after marking an assignment or observing practice. Feedback should help motivate your students and not demoralise them in any way. Ideally, it should be a two-way process allowing for student questions and to clarify points. After making a decision regarding the progress of a student, you would need to decide how to give feedback.

Some different methods of giving feedback include:

- verbal – either on a one-to-one basis, as a group, as part of a review or tutorial, or in front of others, for example, the peer group

- written – on each student's work and/or on a separate feedback record or checklist

- electronically – either by e-mail or part of an online program or web portal

You should choose the right time and place for verbal feedback and allow enough time for your student to ask you questions. Remaining factual and being objective should help reassure, boost confidence, encourage and motivate your students. Feedback should always be given at a level which is appropriate for each student and does not include a lot of jargon. Feedback can be direct, i.e. to an individual, or indirect, i.e. to a group. It should be more thorough than just a quick comment such as 'Well done' and should include specific facts which relate to progress; success or otherwise, in order to help your student develop. You could always ask your student first how they think they have done as it gives them the opportunity to say what errors they might have made before you point them out. If you are giving written or electronic feedback, consider how your student reads it may not be how you intended it to be read. Starting with something positive, moving onto something which needs development and ending on a positive note can help your student remain focused on what you are saying.

At level 4 you could review the ways you have given feedback and state what you would do differently. You might give verbal feedback, but not be aware of how your body language, facial expressions and tone of voice influence the way you are saying it. You would need to take into account any non-verbal signals from your student as you might need to adapt your feedback if you see they are becoming uncomfortable or not taking in what you are saying. If you have given written feedback, you might feel what you have said made sense, but when your student read it they had a few questions. Conversely, you might have given too much feedback, which has confused your student as they are not sure what they have achieved or what to do next.

You could relate your response to theorists such as Skinner (1968) who argued that without immediate feedback, especially when the response is wrong, your student will carry on making the same mistake thinking they are right. They will then have to unlearn their response. Time can be wasted by students unlearning their wrong responses instead of learning new behaviours.

If you are currently teaching, you could state how your organisation expects you to give feedback, for example, writing in the first, second or third person, along with the types of records you would maintain.

You could review the advantages of giving constructive feedback, for example, it:

- creates opportunities for clarification and discussion
- emphasises progress rather than failure
- helps improve confidence and motivation
- identifies further learning opportunities or any action required

If you are currently teaching, you could give an example of how you have put each into practice.

You could review the strengths and limitations of different ways of giving feedback, for example, evaluative and descriptive, constructive and destructive, and objective and subjective.

Theory focus

References and further information

Francis, M and Gould, J (2009) *Achieving your PTLLS Award*. London: Sage Publications Ltd.

Gravells, A (2012) *Preparing to Teach in the Lifelong Learning Sector: The New Award* (5th Edn). London: Learning Matters.

Skinner, BF (1968) *The Technology of Teaching*. New York: Appleton, Century and Crofts.

Websites

Free maths and English training – www.move-on.org.uk

Free ICT training – http://learn.go-on.co.uk/

Giving feedback – http://www.brookes.ac.uk/services/ocsld/firstwords/fw21.html

Ground rules – http://www.learningandteaching.info/teaching/ground_rules.htm

Motivating adults – http://www.assetproject.info/learner_methodologies/before/motivating.htm

UNIT TITLE: Understanding inclusive learning and teaching in lifelong learning

LEVEL 3 (3 credits)

Learning Outcomes The learner will:	Assessment Criteria The learner can:		Example evidence
3. Understand ways to create a motivating learning environment	3.1	Explain ways to engage and motivate learners in an inclusive learning environment	An explanation of how you would engage and motivate your students. *Cross-referenced to the unit: Understanding inclusive learning and teaching in lifelong learning 1.3 and 2.1.*
	3.2	Summarise ways to establish ground rules with learners to promote respect for others	A summary of how to establish ground rules with students. An explanation of how behaviour and respect can be managed by the use of ground rules. A list of possible ground rules relevant to the subject to be taught along with any organisational requirements.
	3.3	Explain ways to give constructive feedback that motivates learners	An explanation of how you would give constructive feedback to your students which retains their motivation. Examples of giving written feedback, i.e. anonomised records.

UNIT TITLE: Understanding inclusive learning and teaching in lifelong learning
LEVEL 4 (3 credits)

Learning Outcomes	Assessment Criteria		Example evidence
The learner will:	The learner can:		
3. Understand how to create a motivating learning environment	3.1	Explain how to engage and motivate learners in an inclusive learning environment	An explanation of how you would engage and motivate your students. *Cross-referenced to the unit: Understanding inclusive learning and teaching in lifelong learning 1.3 and 2.1.*
	3.2	Explain how to establish ground rules with learners to promote respect for others	A detailed explanation of how to establish ground rules with students. An explanation of how behaviour and respect can be managed by the use of ground rules. A list of possible ground rules relevant to the subject to be taught along with any organisational requirements.
	3.3	Review ways to give constructive feedback to motivate learners	A review of how you would give constructive feedback to your students which retains their motivation. A review of the advantages of giving constructive feedback along with examples. A review of the strengths and limitations of different ways of giving feedback. Examples of giving written feedback, i.e. annonmised records. A comparison of relevant feedback theories.

CHAPTER 7
BE ABLE TO PLAN
INCLUSIVE LEARNING AND
TEACHING SESSIONS

This chapter is in two parts. The first part: *Self assessment activities*, contains questions and activities which relate to the first learning outcome of the PTLLS unit *Using inclusive learning and teaching approaches in lifelong learning*.

The assessment criteria for each level are shown in boxes and are followed by questions and activities for you to carry out. Ensure that your responses are *specific to you*, the *subject* you will teach and the *context* and *environment* in which you will teach.

After completing the activities, check your responses with the second part: *Guidance for evidencing achievement*. This guidance is not intended to give you the answers to questions you may be asked in any formal assessments; however, it will help you focus your responses towards meeting the PTLLS assessment criteria.

At the end of each chapter is an example of a completed assessment grid at level 3 and level 4. These give examples of evidence you could provide towards the assessment criteria. Evidence can be cross-referenced between units and assessment criteria if it meets the requirements.

Self assessment activities

> Level 3 – 1.1 Plan a session for learning and teaching that meets the needs of learners
>
> Level 4 – 1.1 Plan a session for learning and teaching that meets the needs of learners

Q31 Create a session plan for a 15- or 30-minute session with students (your PTLLS observer will advise you of the time length). This will be for your own students if you are currently teaching, or for your peers as part of a micro-teach session.

Level 3 – 1.2 Justify the selection of approaches to meet the needs of learners

Level 4 – 1.2 Justify the selection of approaches to meet the needs of learners

Q32 Justify how your selected teaching and learning approaches will meet the needs of your students or your peers.

Level 3 – 1.3 Plan assessment methods to meet the needs of learners

Level 4 – 1.3 Not applicable to level 4

Q33 What assessment methods will you plan to use to meet the needs of your students?

Guidance for evidencing achievement

Level 3 – 1.1 Plan a session for learning and teaching that meets the needs of learners

Level 4 – 1.1 Plan a session for learning and teaching that meets the needs of learners

Q31 Create a session plan for a 15- or 30-minute session with students (your PTLLS observer will advise you of the time length). This will be for your own students if you are currently teaching, or for your peers as part of a micro-teach session.

You should be given a pro-forma or template to use as the basis for your session plan. If you are currently teaching, this should be the one from your organisation. If you are delivering a micro-teach session to your peers, you should be given a suitable plan. You will also be told how long you will deliver your session for, usually 15 or 30 minutes.

You could create a rationale for your session which will state the:

● date, venue and duration of the session

● subject, level, and aim and objectives

● group composition, for example, number of students and how their needs will be met through differentiation, equality and diversity and learning styles

● the teaching and learning approaches to be used

● the activities and resources to be used

● the assessment methods to be used

Your session plan should have a logical beginning, middle and end and take into account differentiation, equality and diversity, individual learning needs and learning styles. You will need to ascertain these details in advance from your students or peer group. Your aim should be stated, this is what you hope to achieve during the session. There should be a clear break-down of what you will do, and what your students will do (the objectives), along with a good mix of activities and assessment opportunities. Timings should be stated, for example, 2.00 pm, 2.05 pm, etc. next to each activity.

Alternatively you could state 5 minutes, 6 minutes, etc. for each activity. You will need to consider what resources you will use, for example, electronic presentation equipment, flip chart paper, interactive whiteboard, pens, handouts, activities, text books, etc.

Your session plan should be realistic, don't attempt to achieve too much from either yourself or your students. Consider an activity you could remove if you run out of time, and also something extra you could add in if you have spare time. It is also useful to have spare activities for students who may finish earlier than others, and extension activities for students who are more able and like challenges. You should also have a contingency plan in case anything goes wrong, such as a hard copy of a computerised presentation, or what to do if you have spare time. Always end your session plan with a summary linking back to your aim and the objectives, and allow time for student questions.

At level 4 your session plan should show innovation and creativity to take into account all your students' individual needs, and how you will differentiate for different levels of ability and learning styles.

Please see Chapter 13 for further information regarding the micro-teach session.

| Level 3 – 1.2 Justify the selection of approaches to meet the needs of learners |
| Level 4 – 1.2 Justify the selection of approaches to meet the needs of learners |

Q32 Justify how your selected teaching and learning approaches will meet the needs of your students or your peers.

Your response could justify how you plan to meet the individual needs of your students. You should obtain details of your students or peer group in advance to ascertain their learning styles and/or any particular needs. It could be that you have a student with dyslexia who might benefit from a pastel coloured background for presentations or handouts. All students can benefit from this rather than singling out and possibly embarrassing one person. Your resources should not create any barriers to learning and should be accessible to all.

You might have students of different abilities or levels within the same group, therefore you will need to state how you will plan different activities to stretch and challenge the higher level students. You could plan to use varied activities, ask open questions, and incorporate individual, paired or group work. If your group contains mainly kinaesthetic students, planning practical activities will help them learn best. However, make sure you use strategies which cover all learning styles to ensure all students benefit.

At level 4, you could relate your response to quotes from text books, for example, *Your choice of teaching strategy is often related to your own individual style and what you feel most comfortable in doing. However ... you might like to consider... what do I want my students to be able to do? – what do I want my students to know?* (Reece and Walker, 2007: 101). You could then state what your style of teaching is and how you will use your planned strategies to ensure your students can demonstrate they do know what they are doing, whether this is to demonstrate a skill, or knowledge and understanding.

You could also justify how you will take aspects such as health and safety and safeguarding into consideration.

> Level 3 – 1.3 Plan assessment methods to meet the needs of learners
>
> Level 4 – 1.3 Not applicable to level 4

Q33 What assessment methods will you plan to use to meet the needs of your students?

This question is not part of the level 4 assessment criteria for this unit.

At level 3, your response should explain the assessment methods you plan to use for your observed session, for example, open questions to test knowledge or observation to see knowledge put into practice. Your methods should be fit for purpose, relate to what has been taught and take into account skills, knowledge and understanding.

You could state how you will use initial, formative and summative types of assessment. Initial assessment can be used at the beginning of the session to ask if anyone has any knowledge of the topic to be taught. (This is different to initial assessment at the commencement of the programme.) You can then include these students during the session by asking them to describe their experiences. (Initial assessment can also be used prior to the session to find out learning styles and any particular learning needs.)

Formative assessment can be ongoing throughout the session via questions and various activities such as group work. Summative assessment can be at the end of the session by use of a quiz or activity to enable you to assess that learning has taken place by everyone for the topic taught.

If you are working towards the unit *Principles of assessment in lifelong learning* you could cross-reference this response to your responses for that unit. Alternatively, your rationale and session plan might contain enough detail to demonstrate your knowledge of assessment during your observed session.

Theory focus

References and further information

Avis, J, Fisher, R and Thompson, R (2011) *Teaching in Lifelong Learning: A Guide To Theory And Practice*. Oxford: Oxford University Press.

Fleming, N (2005) *Teaching and Learning Styles: VARK Strategies*. Honolulu: Honolulu Community College.

Gravells, A (2012) *Preparing to Teach in the Lifelong Learning Sector: The New Award* (5th Edn). London: Learning Matters.

Gravells, A and Simpson, S (2012) *Equality and Diversity in the Lifelong Learning Sector* (2nd Edn). London: Learning Matters.

Reece, I and Walker, S (2007) *Teaching, Training and Learning: A Practical Guide* (6th Edn). Tyne & Wear: Business Education Publishers.

Wallace, S (2011) *Teaching, Tutoring and Training in the Lifelong Learning Sector* (4th Edn). Exeter: Learning Matters.

Williams, J (2012) *Study Skills for PTLLS* (2nd Edn). London: Learning Matters.

Wilson, L (2008) *Practical Teaching A Guide to PTLLS and CTLLS*. London: Cengage Learning.

Websites

Assessment methods – http://www.brookes.ac.uk/services/ocsld/resources/methods.html

Fleming's Learning Styles – www.vark-learn.com

Health & Safety at Work etc Act (1974) – http://www.hse.gov.uk/legislation/hswa.htm

Safeguarding Vulnerable Groups Act (2006) – http://www.opsi.gov.uk/ACTS/acts2006/ukpga_20060047_en_1

Theories of learning – www.learningandteaching.info/learning/

UNIT TITLE: Using inclusive learning and teaching approaches in lifelong learning

LEVEL 3 (3 credits)

Learning Outcomes The learner will:	Assessment Criteria The learner can:		Example evidence
1. Be able to plan inclusive learning and teaching sessions	1.1	Plan a session for learning and teaching that meets the needs of learners	Syllabus or qualification handbook for your subject. Rationale for your session. Session plan showing how individual needs will be met, e.g. differentiation for different levels, abilities, learning styles and individual needs. The plan should have a clear aim of what you want your learners to achieve, with objectives stating what they will do.
	1.2	Justify the selection of approaches to meet the needs of learners	A justification as to the reasons why you have selected your teaching and learning approaches. A justification of how the approaches will meet the needs of your particular students for the session you will deliver. Examples of resources and activities to be used with students, e.g. handouts, presentations, etc.
	1.3	Plan assessment methods to meet the needs of learners	Rationale and session plan showing which assessment methods will be used. An explanation of why the chosen assessment methods will be used. *Cross-referenced to the unit Principles of assessment in lifelong learning.*

UNIT TITLE: Using inclusive learning and teaching approaches in lifelong learning
LEVEL 4 (3 credits)

Learning Outcomes The learner will:	Assessment Criteria The learner can:		Example evidence
1. Be able to plan inclusive learning and teaching sessions	1.1	Plan a session for learning and teaching that meets the needs of learners	See the *guidance for evidencing achievement* for sample explanations which should be produced using academic writing and referencing conventions Syllabus or qualification handbook for your subject. Rationale for your session. Session plan showing how individual needs will be met, e.g. differentiation for different levels, abilities, learning styles and individual needs. The plan should have a clear aim of what you want your learners to achieve, with objectives stating what they will do.
	1.2	Justify the selection of approaches to meet the needs of learners	A justification as to the reasons why you have selected your teaching and learning approaches. A justification of how the approaches will meet the needs of your particular students for the session you will deliver. Examples of resources and activities to be used with students, e.g. handouts, presentations, etc.

CHAPTER 8
BE ABLE TO DELIVER
INCLUSIVE LEARNING AND
TEACHING SESSIONS

This chapter is in two parts. The first part: *Self assessment activities*, contains questions and activities which relate to the second learning outcome of the PTLLS unit *Using inclusive learning and teaching approaches in lifelong learning*.

The assessment criteria for each level are shown in boxes and are followed by questions and activities for you to carry out. Ensure your responses are *specific to you*, the *subject* you will teach and the *context* and *environment* in which you will teach.

After completing the activities, check your responses with the second part: *Guidance for evidencing achievement*. This guidance is not intended to give you the answers to questions you may be asked in any formal assessments; however, it will help you focus your responses towards meeting the PTLLS assessment criteria.

At the end of each chapter is an example of a completed assessment grid at level 3 and level 4. These give examples of evidence you could provide towards the assessment criteria. Evidence can be cross-referenced between units and assessment criteria if it meets the requirements.

Self assessment activities

Please note – the assessment criteria for level 3 and level 4 in this unit do not directly compare. There is an extra assessment criterion at level 4 in this unit.

Level 3 – 2.1 Apply learning and teaching approaches to meet the needs of learners

Level 4 – 2.1 Demonstrate inclusive learning and teaching approaches to engage and motivate learners

Q34 **Deliver your planned session. During the delivery, ensure you use a range of appropriate teaching and learning approaches to engage and motivate your students.**

Level 3 – 2.2 Use resources to meet the needs of learners

Level 4 – 2.2 Demonstrate the use of appropriate resources to support inclusive learning and teaching

Q35 **During the delivery of your session, use resources that meet the needs of your students and support inclusive learning and teaching.**

Level 3 – 2.3 Communicate with learners to meet their needs and aid their understanding

Level 4 – 2.4 Communicate with learners to meet their needs and aid their understanding

Q36 **During the delivery of your session, ensure you effectively communicate with your students.**

Level 4 - 2.3 Use assessment methods to support learning and teaching

Q37 **Level 4 only. During the delivery of your session, use appropriate assessment methods.**

Level 3 – 2.4 Provide constructive feedback to learners

Level 4 – 2.5 Provide constructive feedback to learners

Q38 **During the delivery of your session, provide constructive feedback to your students regarding their progress and development.**

Guidance for evidencing achievement

Level 3 – 2.1 Apply learning and teaching approaches to meet the needs of learners

Level 4 – 2.1 Demonstrate inclusive learning and teaching approaches to engage and motivate learners

Q34 Deliver your planned session. During the delivery, ensure you use a range of appropriate teaching and learning approaches to engage and motivate your students.

This is a practical task which enables you to deliver a session to your current students if you are in-service, or to your peers if you are pre-service. You could take account of your responses in Chapter 7 to put theory into practice. When delivering your session demonstrate confidence, and convey passion and enthusiasm for your subject. Actively engage your students and use a mixture of teaching and learning approaches to retain motivation. To ensure learning has taken place and to support the learning process, use some form of assessment, for example, asking questions or observing practice.

You might be asked to give your observer a copy of your session plan in advance. This will enable them to ask any questions regarding your choice of teaching and learning approaches and how you plan to engage your learners. They will be able to give you feedback regarding the structure of your plan to achieve your aim and the objectives you plan to use.

You will be observed delivering your session and you will receive verbal and written feedback afterwards from your observer.

As evidence for both level 3 and level 4, you could provide your session plan, observation feedback form, and examples of activities and resources used with your students.

Please see Chapter 13 for further information regarding the micro-teach session.

> Level 3 – 2.2 Use resources to meet the needs of learners
>
> Level 4 – 2.2 Demonstrate the use of appropriate resources to support inclusive learning and teaching

Q35 During the delivery of your session, use resources that meet the needs of your students and support inclusive learning and teaching.

This is a practical task which enables you to use resources which meet the needs of your students. The resources you use should support inclusive learning and teaching.

The resources could include electronic presentation equipment, interactive white boards, flip chart paper and pens, specialist equipment, projectors, digital media, books and handouts etc. All resources should be checked in advance to ensure they are inclusive, fit for purpose, safe and fully operational. If you are a pre-service student you will need to arrive early to check the room you will be teaching in and you may need to ask your observer in advance what is available for you to use. If you are planning to use an electronic presentation it would be useful to e-mail this to your observer in advance for them to check it, in case the program you plan to use isn't compatible. You should also have a backup plan in case the computer doesn't work, i.e. a hard copy of your presentation. All resources you use should be relevant to the subject you are teaching and the individual needs of your students.

As evidence for both level 3 and level 4, you could provide your observer's feedback form, and examples of resources you have used with your students.

> Level 3 – 2.3 Communicate with learners to meet their needs and aid their understanding
>
> Level 4 – 2.4 Communicate with learners to meet their needs and aid their understanding

Q36 During the delivery of your session, ensure you effectively communicate with your students.

This is a practical task which enables you to communicate and interact with your students. You should use methods which engage and motivate your students.

You will need to be aware of how you:

- dress, act, speak and portray yourself as a professional

- encourage student engagement and motivation

- limit the use of jargon and technical information

- manage behaviour and disruption

- use non-verbal communication such as body language and eye contact

- use presentation skills and different teaching and learning strategies

- use different questioning techniques

- use skills such as listening, empathy and sympathy

The person observing your session will want to see you demonstrate appropriate communication techniques. This will include setting your group at ease and the way you introduce your session. They will want to see that you are confident and professional and that you deal with any situations as they arise. Using your students' names as your session progresses, for example, when asking questions, helps to include everyone (you will need to plan enough questions). Ensuring all students are playing an active part in group activities also helps. You will need to be aware of your body language, any regional dialects or accents, and the amount of jargon, technical terms or acronyms you use. You might find it helpful to ask your observer for a copy of the observation form beforehand, to see what they will be looking for. Don't be afraid to ask your observer any questions in advance of your session, they are there to help your professional development.

As evidence for both level 3 and level 4, you could provide your observer's feedback form, and completed feedback forms from your peers.

Level 4 – 2.3 Use assessment methods to support learning and teaching

Q37 Level 4 only. During the delivery of your session, use appropriate assessment methods.

This is a practical task enabling level 4 PTLLS students to demonstrate the use of appropriate assessment methods. You could use open questions to test knowledge, i.e. those beginning with who, what, when, where, why or how. You could use observation to see knowledge put into practice through group activities or paired work. You could demonstrate the use of initial assessment at the beginning of the session to ask if anyone has any knowledge of the topic to be taught. You could demonstrate formative assessment through questions and activities which support the topic, and summative by using a quiz or activity to assess knowledge, understanding and/or skills at the end. Whichever methods you use, they should be valid and reliable, and you need to be satisfied that learning has taken place by everyone.

As evidence for level 4, you could provide your observer's feedback, examples of assessment activities used with students and a visual recording if this was used.

Level 3 – 2.4 Provide constructive feedback to learners

Level 4 – 2.5 Provide constructive feedback to learners

Q38 During the delivery of your session, provide constructive feedback to your students regarding their progress and development.

This is a practical task enabling you to demonstrate how you provide constructive feedback to your students. Feedback should confirm achievement or otherwise, be given in a manner that will help your student, and be constructive and developmental. Good feedback can offer guidance and information, it is not a judgement of personality, character or potential. Feedback can be to individuals or groups and can be informal or formal depending upon the situation.

Please see Q30 in Chapter 6 for more information regarding feedback.

As evidence for both level 3 and level 4, you could provide your observer's feedback form, and completed feedback forms from your peers. These should reflect how effective your own feedback was during the session.

Theory focus

References and further information

Avis, J, Fisher, R and Thompson, R (2011) *Teaching in Lifelong Learning: A Guide To Theory And Practice*. Oxford: Oxford University Press.

Hill, C (2008) *Teaching with e-learning in the Lifelong Learning Sector* (2nd Edn). Exeter: Learning Matters.

Gravells, A (2012) *Preparing to Teach in the Lifelong Learning Sector: The New Award* (5th Edn). London: Learning Matters.

IfL (2008) *Code of Professional Practice*. London: Institute for Learning.

Reece, I and Walker, S (2007) *Teaching, Training and Learning: A Practical Guide* (6th Edn). Tyne & Wear: Business Education Publishers.

Wallace, S (2011) *Teaching, Tutoring and Training in the Lifelong Learning Sector* (4th Edn). Exeter: Learning Matters.

Websites

Feedback – http://escalate.ac.uk/4147

Fleming's Learning Styles – www.vark-learn.com

Institute for Learning – www.ifl.ac.uk

Theories of learning and teaching – www.learningandteaching.info/learning/

UNIT TITLE: Using inclusive learning and teaching approaches in lifelong learning
LEVEL 3 (3 credits)

Learning Outcomes	Assessment Criteria		Example evidence
The learner will:	The learner can:		
2. Be able to deliver inclusive learning and teaching sessions	2.1	Apply learning and teaching approaches to meet the needs of learners	Session plan. Observer's feedback form. Examples of activities used.
	2.2	Use resources to meet the needs of learners	Observer's feedback form. Examples of resources used.
	2.3	Communicate with learners to meet their needs and aid their understanding	Observer's feedback form. Completed peer feedback forms (received). Visual recording of session.
	2.4	Provide constructive feedback to learners	Observer's feedback form.

UNIT TITLE: Using inclusive learning and teaching approaches in lifelong learning

LEVEL 4 (3 credits)

Learning Outcomes The learner will:	Assessment Criteria The learner can:		Example evidence
2. Be able to deliver inclusive learning and teaching sessions	2.1	Demonstrate inclusive learning and teaching approaches to engage and motivate learners.	Session plan. Observer's feedback form. Examples of activities used.
	2.2	Demonstrate the use of appropriate resources to support inclusive learning and teaching	Observer's feedback form. Examples of resources used.
	2.3	Use assessment methods to support learning and teaching	Observer's feedback form. Examples of assessment activities used with students.
	2.4	Communicate with learners to meet their needs and aid their understanding	Observer's feedback form. Completed peer feedback forms (received). Visual recording of session.
	2.5	Provide constructive feedback to learners	Observer's feedback form.

CHAPTER 9
BE ABLE TO EVALUATE OWN PRACTICE IN DELIVERING INCLUSIVE LEARNING AND TEACHING

This chapter is in two parts. The first part: **Self assessment activities**, contains questions and activities which relate to the third learning outcome of the PTLLS unit **Using inclusive learning and teaching approaches in lifelong learning**.

The assessment criteria for each level are shown in boxes and are followed by questions and activities for you to carry out. Ensure your responses are *specific to you*, the *subject* you will teach and the *context* and *environment* in which you will teach.

After completing the activities, check your responses with the second part: **Guidance for evidencing achievement**. This guidance is not intended to give you the answers to questions you may be asked in any formal assessments; however, it will help you focus your responses towards meeting the PTLLS assessment criteria.

At the end of each chapter is an example of a completed assessment grid at level 3 and level 4. These give examples of evidence you could provide towards the assessment criteria. Evidence can be cross-referenced between units and assessment criteria if it meets the requirements.

Self assessment activities

Level 3 – 3.1 Reflect on own approaches to delivering inclusive learning and teaching

Level 4 – 3.1 Review own approaches to delivering inclusive learning and teaching

Q39 After you have delivered your session, reflect on (level 3) or review (level 4) the approaches you used.

Level 3 – 3.2 Identify areas for improvement in own practice

Level 4 – 3.2 Analyse how own inclusive learning and teaching practice can be improved to meet the needs of learners

Q40 After you have delivered your session, identify (level 3) or analyse (level 4) the improvements you could make, for yourself and your students.

Guidance for evidencing achievement

Level 3 – 3.1 Reflect on own approaches to delivering inclusive learning and teaching

Level 4 – 3.1 Review own approaches to delivering inclusive learning and teaching

Q39 After you have delivered your session, reflect on (level 3) or review (level 4) the approaches you used.

Your response could reflect upon the different approaches you used when you delivered your session. You could give examples of what you used and how effective, or not, they were. For example, you might have felt that using a discussion was lively and generated a good debate; however, not every student contributed. Next time, you would ensure you involved each student in some way, perhaps by restructuring groups to ensure everyone is taking part, or by asking individual questions.

You might have been given a *self-evaluation form* to complete after your session, or you might be maintaining an ongoing reflective learning journal. Before completing these, consider how your session went. You might think your session was successful; however, you need to take into account the feedback you have received from your observer and your peers before making a decision. If your session was visually recorded, watch it to help you see how you appear to others, for example, how you speak or react to different situations. You might be surprised to see things you didn't know you did.

Reflecting on your teaching includes thinking about what you have done and how you could improve or modify it for the future. You might think everything has gone well, if this is the case, consider *why* it went well to see if you could use the techniques again. Evaluating the effectiveness of your own teaching includes making a decision as to how successful the session was and how successful you were at facilitating learning. For example, you might state that you felt the session was a success as your students were able to answer all the questions you asked, or demonstrate a skill. However, if not all students were given the opportunity to answer a question or demonstrate a skill, you won't know if they have learnt anything.

At level 4 you could review the approaches you used, for example, stating your strengths and limitations.

Example – strengths:

- being prepared and setting up the area/checking all equipment in advance
- giving a clear introduction of yourself, and the aim of the session
- using a variety of resources
- using students' names
- displaying positive body language
- summarising the aim
- clearing up afterwards

Example – limitations:

- not asking every student an open question to check knowledge
- not keeping to the session plan timings, which resulted in time to spare at the end
- giving a handout too early

You could then expand on each of the above to say *why* they did or did not contribute towards an effective and inclusive session.

If you have been maintaining a diary or reflective learning journal through-out your time taking the PTLLS Award, you could cross-reference your response to them. You could also relate your journal entries and written responses to reflective theorists such as: Brookfield (1995), Gibbs (1998), Griffiths and Tann (1992), Kolb (1984), Schön (1983) and others. You might wish to compare and contrast the different theories to demonstrate your knowledge at this level.

Level 3 – 3.2 Identify areas for improvement in own practice

Level 4 – 3.2 Analyse how own inclusive learning and teaching practice can be improved to meet the needs of learners

---

Q40 After you have delivered your session, identify (level 3) or analyse (level 4) the improvements you could make, for yourself and your students.

Your response could identify the areas you feel you could improve.

Example – self:

- asking if anyone has any knowledge of the subject at the beginning of the session
- not giving a handout part way through as it disrupted the group
- using eye contact with all students
- trying not to say 'erm', 'yeah' and 'okay'
- keeping jargon to a minimum
- offering to e-mail a copy of the presentation to everyone

Example – students:

- enabling students to work in smaller groups
- using paired activities and peer assessment
- using differentiated activities to stretch and challenge higher level students
- having an extra activity for students if there is spare time

You could create an action plan for your own development. You might wish to attend a literacy session to help improve your spelling, or arrange to be taught how to use an interactive white board. You could observe an experienced teacher in the same subject area as your own, and carry out further research and reading regarding the areas you wish to improve.

At level 4 you could analyse the above and describe *how* you knew why something didn't work and *what* you will do next time to ensure it does. You can then analyse how your own learning and teaching practice can be improved to meet the needs of your students.

For example:

I would give a handout at the end so as not to disrupt the group during the session. I found the students fiddled with it and started reading it as soon as I gave it out and they didn't pay attention to what I was saying.

I was very focused upon keeping to the timings of my session plan so that I kept looking at it rather than my students. I need to use more eye contact with my students as this would enable me to observe that they are watching what I am doing, and enable them to see that I am paying attention to them.

I found that three students in the group were able to complete the activity with ease and very quickly. Next time I will create two different versions of the activity so that one can be aimed at challenging the higher level students further.

I couldn't give everyone a copy of the presentation as the photocopier wasn't working prior to the session. If I offer to e-mail a copy to everyone it will give them the opportunity to look at it in their own time and also address issues of sustainability. In future, I will either aim to get copies done sooner so that I am better prepared, or agree with the students to use electronic ones to help the environment.

You could relate your response to quotes from text books, for example, *Often just thinking about a situation can help you feel differently about something when you attempt to place things into context. Acknowledging that you are not personally responsible for every little thing and everybody can be a useful and enlightening experience for some* (Roffey-Barentsen and Malthouse, 2009: 24). You could then state how this quote has impacted upon your own reflection and improvement.

Theory focus

References and further information

Brookfield, SD (1995) *Becoming a Critically Reflective Teacher.* San Francisco, CA: Jossey-Bass.

Gibbs, G (1988) *Learning by Doing: A Guide to Teaching and Learning Methods.* Oxford: Further Education Unit.

Gravells, A (2012) *Preparing to Teach in the Lifelong Learning Sector: The New Award* (5th Edn). London: Learning Matters.

Griffiths, M and Tann, S (1992) Using reflective practice to link personal and public theories. *Journal of Education for Teaching,* Vol 18, No 1.

Kolb, DA (1984) *Experiential Learning: Experience as the Source of Learning and Development.* New Jersey: Prentice-Hall.

Reece, I and Walker, S (2007) *Teaching, Training and Learning; A Practical Guide* (6th Edn). Tyne & Wear: Business Education Publishers Ltd.

Roffey-Barentsen, J and Malthouse, R (2009) *Reflective Practice in the Lifelong Learning Sector* (2nd Edn). Exeter: Learning Matters.

Schön, D (1983) *The Reflective Practitioner.* San Francisco, CA: Jossey-Bass.

Wallace, S (2011) *Teaching, Tutoring and Training in the Lifelong Learning Sector* (4th Edn). Exeter: Learning Matters.

Williams, J (2012) *Study Skills for PTLLS* (2nd Edn). London: Learning Matters.

Websites

Reflective practice – http://www.learningandteaching.info/learning/reflecti.htm

UNIT TITLE: Using inclusive learning and teaching approaches in lifelong learning
LEVEL 3 (3 credits)

Learning Outcomes	Assessment Criteria		Example evidence
The learner will:	The learner can:		
3. Be able to evaluate own practice in delivering inclusive learning and teaching	3.1	Reflect on own approaches to delivering inclusive learning and teaching	A reflection of the different approaches you used and how effective they were. Completed self-evaluation form. Reflective learning journals. Observer and peer feedback.
	3.2	Identify areas for improvement in own practice	An identification of what you could improve for yourself and your students. Action plan for own development.

UNIT TITLE: Using inclusive learning and teaching approaches in lifelong learning

LEVEL 4 (3 credits)

Learning Outcomes The learner will:	Assessment Criteria The learner can:		Example evidence
3. Be able to evaluate own practice in delivering inclusive learning and teaching	3.1	Review own approaches to delivering inclusive learning and teaching	A review of the different approaches you used and how effective they were. A list of own strengths of limitations. Completed self-evaluation form. Reflective learning journals. A comparison of reflective theories. Observer and peer feedback.
	3.2	Analyse how own inclusive learning and teaching practice can be improved to meet the needs of learners	An identification of what you could improve for yourself and your students. Action plan for own development. Evidence of continuing professional development (CPD).

This chapter is in two parts. The first part: **Self assessment activities**, contains questions and activities which relate to the first learning outcome of the PTLLS unit **Principles of assessment in lifelong learning**.

The assessment criteria for each level are shown in boxes and are followed by questions and activities for you to carry out. Ensure your responses are *specific to you*, the *subject* you will teach and the *context* and *environment* in which you will teach.

After completing the activities, check your responses with the second part: **Guidance for evidencing achievement**. This guidance is not intended to give you the answers to questions you may be asked in any formal assessments; however, it will help you focus your responses towards meeting the PTLLS assessment criteria.

At the end of each chapter is an example of a completed assessment grid at level 3 and level 4. These give examples of evidence you could provide towards the assessment criteria. Evidence can be cross-referenced between units and assessment criteria if it meets the requirements.

If you have achieved, or are currently working towards an acceptable Assessor qualification, you might be exempt from taking one or more of the learning outcomes for the unit *Principles of Assessment in Lifelong Learning*. You will need to discuss this with your assessor.

Self assessment activities

> Level 3 – 1.1 Explain types of assessment used in lifelong learning
>
> Level 4 – 1.1 Analyse how types of assessment are used in lifelong learning

Q41 Explain (level 3) or analyse (level 4) types of assessment.

> Level 3 – 1.2 Explain the use of methods of assessment in lifelong learning
>
> Level 4 – 1.2 Analyse how assessment methods are used in lifelong learning

Q42 Explain (level 3) or analyse (level 4) methods of assessment.

> Level 3 – 1.3 Compare the strengths and limitations of assessment methods to meet individual learner needs
>
> Level 4 – 1.3 Evaluate strengths and limitations of assessment methods to meet individual learner needs

Q43 Compare (level 3) or evaluate (level 4) the strengths and limitations of assessment methods to meet individual student needs.

Guidance for evidencing achievement

Level 3 – 1.1 Explain types of assessment used in lifelong learning

Level 4 – 1.1 Analyse how types of assessment are used in lifelong learning

Q41 Explain (level 3) or analyse (level 4) types of assessment.

Your response could explain that types of assessment include *initial* (at the beginning), *formative* (ongoing to inform progress), and *summative* (at the end to confirm skills, knowledge and/or understanding). An example of an initial assessment could be to ascertain prior knowledge of a topic. An example of formative assessment could be an ongoing learning journal, and a summative assessment could be a test, assignment or an exam.

Diagnostic assessment could be used to ascertain information regarding literacy, numeracy or ICT skills. It can also be used to ascertain skills and knowledge, perhaps by observation and questioning to confirm current competence and understanding.

Assessments can be *formal*, for example, a test, or *informal*, for example a quiz, depending upon your subject and whether the activity is formative or summative. Assessment tasks or activities will be either *internal* (produced by you or your organisation) or *external* (produced by the Awarding Organisation).

At level 4 you could analyse how you use the types mentioned above in different situations. For example, using initial assessments helps you to identify any particular aspects which might otherwise go unnoticed. Some students may be embarrassed or not wish to divulge personal information on application or initial assessment forms. You could have a quiet chat with them away from other students to find out if they have any needs or specific requirements. If you are unsure about how to help them with anything, just ask, as they are best placed to know how you could support them. Initial assessment can also include identifying appropriate learning styles, and ascertaining current skills and knowledge. If you are currently teaching, your organisation may have specific assessments or skills tests for you to use which you could explain, along with how you will use them.

You could also relate your response to quotes from text books, for example, *Assessment types are different from assessment methods. A method is how the assessment type will be used and can be formal or informal. Formal methods count towards the achievement of a qualification whereas informal methods check ongoing progress* (Gravells, 2012a: 31). You could then analyse how you would use different types of assessment in formal and informal situations to suit your particular student needs.

> Level 3 – 1.2 Explain the use of methods of assessment in lifelong learning
>
> Level 4 – 1.2 Analyse how assessment methods are used in lifelong learning

Q42 Explain (level 3) or analyse (level 4) methods of assessment.

Your response could explain the different methods of assessment that can be used for your particular subject. You could list the assessment methods and explain how you would use them. A few examples are given here.

Assignments	Can be used to formally assess progress. Can assess knowledge and understanding and if structured well can allow for assessment of practice.
Observation	Can be used to see students perform a task or skill, putting theory into practice.
Oral questions	A key technique for assessing understanding and stimulating thinking, can be formal or informal. Can be carried out on a one-to-one basis or in group situations. Questions can be closed, hypothetical, open, probing, multiple choice, etc. Can be used to assess knowledge informally during a session or formally as part of an assignment.
Puzzles and quizzes	A fun way of assessing learning in an informal way. Can be used as an informal activity at the end of a session to test knowledge gained, can also be used to fill in time during a session if necessary.

At level 4 you could analyse each of the assessment methods you have stated. This will include explaining *what* the method is, *why*, *when* and *where* you would use it, and *how* both you and your students will benefit from it. For example, assignments could be used to help students provide evidence of knowledge and skills. An assignment can enable the assessment of several aspects of a qualification at the same time, often known as holistic assessment or practice. Perhaps a short assignment could be carried out during the session, and a longer assignment over a few sessions or as homework.

All assessments, whether produced by yourself or others, should be valid and reliable. Validity will ensure you are assessing what is meant to be assessed and reliability will ensure that if the assessment was used again with a similar group of students, you would receive similar results. Most assessments will be internally and/or externally quality assured to ensure fairness and consistency, as well as validity and reliability.

At level 4 you could relate your response to quotes from text books. For example, *One way of solving the curriculum coverage problem is to set a multiple-choice questionnaire. With a questionnaire, it is possible to cover a large body of knowledge or understanding quickly and thoroughly, simply by setting at least one question for each topic covered in the syllabus* (Tummons, 2011: 52). You could then analyse how you would use multiple-choice questions with your own students.

> Level 3 – 1.3 Compare the strengths and limitations of assessment methods to meet individual learner needs
>
> Level 4 – 1.3 Evaluate strengths and limitations of assessment methods to meet individual learner needs

Q43 Compare (level 3) or evaluate (level 4) the strengths and limitations of assessment methods to meet individual student needs.

Your response could compare the strengths and limitations of the assessment methods you have explained in your response to Q42. You might compare the use of an assignment informally and formally. For example, an informal assignment might enable students to work together in a group, whereas a formal assignment must be completed individually. You should take into account any individual needs, for example, a student with dyslexia could complete an assignment using a word processor with a spell check facility. A student with a hearing impairment could write responses to written questions rather than respond verbally to oral questions. You would need to obtain authorisation from your Awarding Organisation before making any changes to formal assessment methods.

You could create a table to compare the strengths and limitations of each of your methods.

A few examples are given here.

Method	Strengths	Limitations
Assignments	Consolidates learning. Several aspects of a qualification can be assessed (holistic assessment). Some assignments are set by the Awarding Organisation who will give clear marking criteria.	Everything must have been taught beforehand. Questions can be misinterpreted if written by someone else. Can be time consuming. Must be individually assessed and written feedback given. Assessor might be biased when marking.
Observations	Enables skills to be seen in action. Students can make a mistake (if it is safe) enabling them to realise their errors. Can assess several aspects of a qualification at the same time (holistic assessment).	Timing must be arranged to suit each student. Communication needs to take place with others (if applicable). No permanent record unless visually recorded. Questions must be asked to confirm understanding. Assessor might not be objective with decision. Student might put on an act for the assessor which isn't how they normally perform.
Puzzles and quizzes	Fun activities to test knowledge, skills and/or attitudes. Useful backup activity if students finish an activity earlier than planned. Useful way to assess progress of lower level students. Good for assessing retention of facts.	Can seem trivial to mature students. Does not assess a student's level of understanding or ability to apply their knowledge to real situations. Can be time consuming to create.

Oral questions	Can be multiple choice, short answer or long essay style. Can challenge and promote a student's potential. A question bank can be devised which could be used again and again for all students. Can test critical arguments or thinking and reasoning skills. Oral questions suit some students more than others, e.g. a dyslexic student might prefer to talk through their responses.	Closed questions only give a yes or no response which doesn't demonstrate knowledge. Questions must be written carefully, i.e. be unambiguous, and can be time consuming to prepare. Expected responses or grading criteria need to be produced beforehand to ensure consistency and validity of judgments. May need to re-phrase some questions if students are struggling with an answer.

At level 4 you could evaluate the strengths and limitations of assessment methods in other ways. For example, internally set and marked assignments versus externally set and marked assignments. This could affect subjectivity and objectivity, if you produce the assignment yourself you might feel you want it to be easy to enable your students to pass first time. If someone else has written the assignment and you are to mark it, you might misinterpret the requirements.

If you are currently teaching, you could produce a case study regarding particular assessment methods you have used to meet individual student needs.

Theory focus

References and further information

Gravells, A (2012a) *Achieving your TAQA Assessor and Internal Quality Assurer Award*. London: Learning Matters.

Gravells, A (2012b) *Preparing to Teach in the Lifelong Learning Sector: The New Award* (5th Edn). London: Learning Matters.

Read, H (2011) *The Best Assessor's Guide*. Bideford: Read On Publications.

Tummons, J (2011) *Assessing Learning in the Lifelong Learning Sector* (3rd Edn). Exeter: Learning Matters.

Websites

Assessment methods – http://www.brookes.ac.uk/services/ocsld/resources/methods.html

UNIT TITLE: Principles of assessment in lifelong learning

LEVEL 3 (3 credits)

Learning Outcomes	Assessment Criteria		Example evidence
The learner will:	The learner can:		
1. Understand types and methods of assessment used in lifelong learning	1.1	Explain types of assessment used in lifelong learning	An explanation of different types of assessment.
	1.2	Explain the use of methods of assessment in lifelong learning	An explanation of different assessment methods and how they could be used with students. Examples of assessment activities used with students.
	1.3	Compare the strengths and limitations of assessment methods to meet individual learner needs	A comparison of the strengths and limitations of various assessment methods. An explanation of how assessment methods can meet individual student needs.

UNIT TITLE: Principles of assessment in lifelong learning
LEVEL 4 (3 credits)

Learning Outcomes The learner will:	Assessment Criteria The learner can:		Example evidence
1. Understand how types and methods of assessment are used in lifelong learning	1.1	Analyse how types of assessment are used in lifelong learning	An analysis of how different types of assessment are used.
	1.2	Analyse how assessment methods are used in lifelong learning	An analysis of different assessment methods and how they could be used with students. Examples of assessment activities.
	1.3	Evaluate strengths and limitations of assessment methods to meet individual learner needs	An evaluation of the strengths and limitations of various assessment methods. A case study of how assessment methods can meet individual student needs.

CHAPTER 11
UNDERSTAND WAYS TO INVOLVE LEARNERS IN THE ASSESSMENT PROCESS

This chapter is in two parts. The first part: **Self assessment activities**, contains questions and activities which relate to the second learning outcome of the PTLLS unit **Principles of assessment in lifelong learning**.

The assessment criteria for each level are shown in boxes and are followed by questions and activities for you to carry out. Ensure your responses are *specific to you*, the *subject* you will teach and the *context* and *environment* in which you will teach.

After completing the activities, check your responses with the second part: **Guidance for evidencing achievement**. This guidance is not intended to give you the answers to questions you may be asked in any formal assessments; however, it will help you focus your responses towards meeting the PTLLS assessment criteria.

At the end of each chapter is an example of a completed assessment grid at level 3 and level 4. These give examples of evidence you could provide towards the assessment criteria. Evidence can be cross-referenced between units and assessment criteria if it meets the requirements.

Self assessment activities

> Level 3 – 2.1 Explain ways to involve the learner in the assessment process
>
> Level 4 – 2.1 Evaluate how to involve the learner in the assessment process

Q44 Explain (level 3) or evaluate (level 4) the ways you could involve your students throughout the assessment process.

> Level 3 – 2.2 Explain the role of peer and self-assessment in the assessment process
>
> Level 4 – 2.2 Analyse the role of peer and self-assessment in the assessment process

Q45 Explain (level 3) or analyse (level 4) the role of peer and self-assessment in the assessment process

Guidance for evidencing achievement

Level 3 – 2.1 Explain ways to involve the learner in the assessment process

Level 4 – 2.1 Evaluate how to involve the learner in the assessment process

Q44 Explain (level 3) or evaluate (level 4) the ways you could involve your students throughout the assessment process.

Your response could explain that initial assessment will help identify any particular student needs and learning styles. Diagnostic assessment will help identify your students' skills, knowledge and understanding towards the subject, and their literacy, numeracy and ICT skills. Your students will be involved from the start, or even before they commence the programme, to help identify these points. It might be that one of your students has already achieved a unit or some of the qualification requirements elsewhere. You could ascertain if they have any evidence of this, i.e. a certificate, so that you could instigate the process of recognising prior learning (RPL).

You can involve your students at the commencement of a session by asking them if they have any prior knowledge or skills of the topic to be covered. In this way, you can draw and build upon their experiences throughout the session.

During the session, you could use paired and group activities which require peer and self-assessment. This would actively involve your students; however, you would need to ensure everyone was aware of the criteria to be assessed, and how to give feedback effectively.

At the end of the session you could informally assess knowledge gained by using a quiz. This would involve the students and end the session on a fun note.

If you are agreeing individual assessment plans with students, for example, if they are to be assessed in the workplace, you would involve them by discussing what will be assessed, how and when. This would enable a two-way conversation to take place, leading to an appropriate plan of action.

Depending upon the topic you are assessing, there are ways of involving your student throughout the process. If you are assessing informally, for example, asking questions during a session, you could start with an open question and move onto a hypothetical question if you are not getting the response you expected. This would help your student think about what they have said.

If you are formally assessing a student for a practical skill, you could ask them open questions to check their understanding. You would not be able to lead your student, but you could probe further to obtain a more detailed response. At the end of the assessment activity, you could ask them how they felt it went. This involves them again and allows them to point out anything that didn't go quite well, before you have to. You could then explain your decision and give constructive feedback, involving your student again by asking them questions and encouraging them to ask you questions.

At level 4 you could evaluate how you would involve your students in the assessment process by beginning with a review of the strengths and limitations of each process.

Process	Strengths of student involvement	Limitations of student involvement
Initial assessment	Can give the student an opportunity to discuss any concerns. Could be carried out electronically.	Student might be apprehensive about taking written, oral or practical tests.
Recognising prior learning (RPL)	Ideal for students who have achieved aspects of the programme or qualification prior to commencement. No need for students to duplicate work, or be reassessed. Values previous achievements.	Checking the authenticity and currency of the evidence provided is crucial. Can be time consuming for both student to prove, and the assessor to assess.

You could then relate your response to quotes from relevant text books, for example, *It could be that you have a learner who has achieved an aspect of a qualification or programme elsewhere. Depending upon the evidence they can produce in support of it, they might not have to repeat some or all the requirements* (Gravells, 2012a: 62).

If you are currently teaching, you could produce a case study evaluating the different assessment methods you have used.

> Level 3 – 2.2 Explain the role of peer and self-assessment in the assessment process
>
> Level 4 – 2.2 Analyse the role of peer and self-assessment in the assessment process

Q45 Explain (level 3) or analyse (level 4) the role of peer and self-assessment in the assessment process.

Your response could explain that peer assessment involves a student assessing another student's progress. Self-assessment involves a student assessing their own progress, which can lead to setting their own goals and targets. It can give responsibility and ownership of their achievements. Both methods encourage students to make decisions about what has been learnt so far, and to reflect on aspects for further development. However, both students and their peers might undervalue or overvalue their achievements. Your students will need to fully understand the assessment criteria, and how to be fair and objective with their judgements. Throughout the process of peer and self-assessment, students can develop skills such as listening, observing and questioning.

Peer assessment can also be useful to develop and motivate students. You would need to give advice to your students as to how to give feedback effectively. If student feedback is given skilfully, other students may consider more what their peers have said than what you have. If you consider peer assessment has a valuable contribution to make to the assessment process, ensure you plan for it, to enable your students to become accustomed and more proficient at giving it. The final decision as to whether your student has achieved will lie with you.

At level 4 you could analyse the role of peer and self-assessment in different situations, for example, peer assessment after a student's presentation. You would need to manage the situation carefully, as you may have some students who do not get along and might use the opportunity to demoralise others. Peer assessment might also take place on occasions when you are not present. You could therefore relate your response to quotes from relevant text books, such as *you can use other learners if, for example, they observed your learner... However, you need to be sure that their accounts are reliable and authentic* (Read, 2011: 75). You could then state how you would ensure the reliability and authenticity of the peer feedback.

You could analyse the advantages and limitations of peer and self-assessment. A couple of examples for each are given here:

Peer assessment advantages:	Peer assessment limitations:
It can reduce the amount of teacher assessment It promotes student and peer interaction and involvement	All peers should be involved, therefore planning needs to take place as to who will give feedback and to whom Appropriate conditions and environment are needed
Self-assessment advantages:	**Self-assessment limitations:**
It encourages students to check their own progress It promotes student involvement and personal responsibility	Assessor needs to discuss and confirm progress and achievement Students may feel they have achieved more than they actually have

Theory focus

References and further information

Gravells, A (2012a) *Achieving your TAQA Assessor and Internal Quality Assurer Award*. London: Learning Matters.

Gravells, A (2012b) *Preparing to Teach in the Lifelong Learning Sector: The New Award* (5th Edn). London: Learning Matters.

Murphy, P (2005) *Learners, Learning and Assessment*. London: Sage.

Read, H (2011) *The Best Assessor's Guide*. Bideford: Read On Publications.

Tummons, J (2011) *Assessing Learning in the Lifelong Learning Sector* (3rd Edn). Exeter: Learning Matters.

Websites

Initial assessment – http://archive.excellencegateway.org.uk/page.aspx?o=108146

Assessment methods – http://www.brookes.ac.uk/services/ocsld/resources/methods.html

UNIT TITLE: Principles of assessment in lifelong learning

LEVEL 3 (3 credits)

Learning Outcomes The learner will:	Assessment Criteria The learner can:		Example evidence
2. Understand ways to involve learners in the assessment process	2.1	Explain ways to involve the learner in the assessment process	An explanation of ways of involving your students throughout the assessment process.
	2.2	Explain the role of peer and self-assessment in the assessment process	An explanation of the role of peer and self-assessment in the assessment process.

UNIT TITLE: Principles of assessment in lifelong learning

LEVEL 4 (3 credits)

Learning Outcomes The learner will:	Assessment Criteria The learner can:		Example evidence
2. Understand how to involve learners in the assessment process	2.1	Evaluate how to involve the learner in the assessment process	An evaluation of how you would involve your students throughout the assessment process. A review of the strengths and limitations of each. A case study regarding how you involved students in the different assessment processes.
	2.2	Analyse the role of peer and self-assessment in the assessment process	An analysis of the role of peer and self-assessment in the assessment process. An analysis of the advantages and limitations of peer and self-assessment.

CHAPTER 12
UNDERSTAND REQUIREMENTS FOR KEEPING RECORDS OF ASSESSMENT IN LIFELONG LEARNING

This chapter is in two parts. The first part: *Self assessment activities*, contains questions and activities which relate to the third learning outcome of the PTLLS unit *Principles of assessment in lifelong learning*.

The assessment criteria for each level are shown in boxes and are followed by questions and activities for you to carry out. Ensure your responses are *specific to you*, the *subject* you will teach and the *context* and *environment* in which you will teach.

After completing the activities, check your responses with the second part: *Guidance for evidencing achievement*. This guidance is not intended to give you the answers to questions you may be asked in any formal assessments; however, it will help you focus your responses towards meeting the PTLLS assessment criteria.

At the end of each chapter is an example of a completed assessment grid at level 3 and level 4. These give examples of evidence you could provide towards the assessment criteria. Evidence can be cross-referenced between units and assessment criteria if it meets the requirements.

Self assessment activities

Level 3 – 3.1 Explain the need to keep records of assessment of learning

Level 4 – 3.1 Explain the need to keep records of assessment of learning

Q46 List the assessment records that a teacher should keep.

Q47 Explain the reasons why these particular records should be kept.

Level 3 – 3.2 Summarise the requirements for keeping records of assessment in an organisation

Level 4 – 3.2 Summarise the requirements for keeping records of assessment in an organisation

Q48 Summarise the requirements for keeping records of assessment in an organisation.

Guidance for evidencing achievement

Level 3 – 3.1 Explain the need to keep records of assessment of learning

Level 4 – 3.1 Explain the need to keep records of assessment of learning

Q46 List the assessment records that a teacher should keep.

Your response could list the assessment records that you would keep, such as:

• action plans	• learning support records
• appeals	• register or record of attendance
• assessment plans	• retention, achievement and
• assessment feedback	progression records
• assessment decisions and grades	• risk assessments
• assessment tracking	• scheme of work
• diagnostic test results	• session plan
• individual learning plans	• skills' audits
• initial assessments	• syllabus or qualification handbook
• interview records	• tutorial reviews
• learning styles tests	

You could also list any others you use or plan to use for your specific subject and the context within which you will assess.

If you are currently assessing students, you could include completed examples of assessment records you have used (anonomised).

At level 4, you could explain in more detail about each document you have listed, i.e. when they are completed and by whom.

Q47 Explain the reasons why these particular records should be kept.

Your response could explain the reasons why you keep particular assessment records, such as to keep track of student achievements, for internal and external audits, and for quality assurance purposes.

If you are currently teaching, you could find out what assessment records your organisation expects you to use and state how you would use them. The syllabus or qualification handbook will give you specific details regarding the assessment strategy; however, they may not provide the assessment documentation you will use to ensure you keep formal records. You could explain how you use the various records (whether manual and/or electronic) along with the advantages and limitations of each. You could also explain how records at your organisation are kept confidential and stored securely and safely.

You could take each of the records you have listed in your response to Q46 and explain why you need to keep them. A few examples are given here:

Record	Reason kept
Action plans	A formal record of agreement with the student which sets out what will be achieved, where, when and how. Sometimes forms part of a learning agreement or contract.
Assessment tracking	To give a visual overview of the progress of each student towards a particular topic, programme or unit.

At level 4, you could explain the strengths and limitations of each, for example:

Record	Strengths	Limitations
Action plans	Can be amended and renegotiated as necessary. Can be individual to each student.	Can be time consuming to agree with every student. Hard copies could be lost. Electronic copies might not always be accessible. Needs to be regularly updated.
Assessment tracking	Can be updated as soon as a student has achieved something, e.g. a unit. A quick way of seeing each student's progress towards the programme or qualification.	Hard copies could be lost. Electronic copies might not always be accessible. Need to be regularly updated.

Level 3 – 3.2 Summarise the requirements for keeping records of assessment in an organisation

Level 4 - 3.2 Summarise the requirements for keeping records of assessment in an organisation

Q48 Summarise the requirements for keeping records of assessment in an organisation.

You might have already addressed this question as part of your response to Q47 as the assessment criteria are very similar.

If not, your response could summarise the requirements, for example internal and external. Internal might include the requirements of the organisation, such as: policies; performance indicators; statistics and data, and quality assurance. External might include the requirements of inspectors, legislation, regulators, professional bodies and funding bodies.

Records can either be electronic or manual and should be kept for a minimum of three years. If you didn't keep assessment records and a student lost their work, you wouldn't have any proof you had planned for and assessed their efforts, unless you kept relevant records.

You could be specific about each record you listed in your response to Q46, i.e. by stating whether it is kept due to organisational, inspection, regulatory or for other requirements. You could then give an instance of why the particular record is kept, for example, an action plan is kept as a requirement of the organisation's assessment policy. If students are taking a qualification, it will also be a requirement of the Awarding Organisation they are registered with.

At level 4 you could relate your response to the Data Protection Act (2003), which made provision for the regulation of the processing of information relating to individuals, including the obtaining, holding, use or disclosure of such information. The amendment in 2003 to the 1998 Data Protection Act included reference to electronic data.

You could also relate your response to quotes from relevant text books, for example, *there are many other organisations and individuals (employers, awarding bodies, admission tutors) who need to know about the achievement of our learners, for a variety of reasons* (Tummons, 2011: 74). You could then summarise the specific organisations which require you to keep records.

Theory focus

References and further information

Gravells, A (2012) *Achieving your TAQA Assessor and Internal Quality Assurer Award*. London: Learning Matters.

Murphy, P (2005) *Learners, Learning and Assessment*. London: SAGE.

Read, H (2011) *The Best Assessor's Guide*. Bideford: Read On Publications.

Tummons, J (2011) *Assessing Learning in the Lifelong Learning Sector* (3rd Edn). Exeter: Learning Matters.

Websites

Data Protection Act (2003) – http://regulatorylaw.co.uk/Data_Protection_Act_2003.html

UNIT TITLE: Principles of assessment in lifelong learning

LEVEL 3 (3 credits)

Learning Outcomes	Assessment Criteria		Example evidence
The learner will:	The learner can:		See the guidance for *evidencing achievement* for sample explanations
3. Understand requirements for keeping records of assessment in lifelong learning	3.1	Explain the need to keep records of assessment of learning	A list of assessment records with an explanation as to why they are used. Examples of records used (anonomised).
	3.2	Summarise the requirements for keeping records of assessment in an organisation	A summary of the reasons why records must be maintained, e.g. organisational, legislative and external requirements.

UNIT TITLE: Principles of assessment in lifelong learning

LEVEL 4 (3 credits)

Learning Outcomes	Assessment Criteria		Example evidence
The learner will:	The learner can:		See the guidance for *evidencing achievement* for sample explanations
3. Understand requirements for keeping records of assessment in lifelong learning	3.1	Explain the need to keep records of assessment of learning	A list of assessment records with an explanation as to why they are used. Examples of records used (anonomised). Strengths and limitations of various assessment records.
	3.2	Summarise the requirements for keeping records of assessment in an organisation	A summary of the reasons why records must be maintained, e.g. organisational, legislative and external requirements.

Introduction

In this chapter you will learn about:

- planning and preparing your micro-teach session
- giving and receiving feedback
- evaluating your micro-teach session
- micro-teaching hints and tips.

Planning and preparing your micro-teach session

To demonstrate your skills and knowledge as a teacher you are required to deliver a session either to your peers (pre-service) or in your place of work (in-service). This gives you the opportunity to put theory into practice. It will usually be for a minimum of 15 or 30 minutes and you will be formally observed. The date and time should be agreed in advance of your session. Your observer might make a visual recording of your session, which you can view in your own time. This will enable you to see things you were not aware of, for example, saying 'erm', using a lot of hand gestures or not using much eye contact. You should be told in advance if you are to be recorded, try not to be put off by it, but embrace it as a way of developing yourself further.

You will need to prepare a session plan in advance, which should have a clear aim (what you want your students to achieve), which is then broken down into objectives (how your students will achieve your aim). Objectives should be measurable to enable you to see that learning has taken place. The term *learning outcomes* is used for qualifications on the QCF, these are an expression of what your student *can do* once learning has taken place and may take longer in terms of time than objectives.

Objectives should always be SMART:

- **S**pecific – are they clearly defined?

- **M**easurable – can they be met?

- **A**chievable – are they possible?

- **R**ealistic – do they relate to the aim?

- **T**ime bound – can they be met in the time?

Examples of SMART objectives include: create, demonstrate, describe, explain and state. These enable you to assess whether your students have gained the required knowledge and/or skills, for example, *students will demonstrate how to fold a napkin*.

You will need to design in advance any activities, handouts, resources, presentations and assessment activities you will use. Make sure these are relevant to your aim and meet the objectives you want your students to achieve. You should also check written resources for spelling, grammar and punctuation errors, and ensure text and pictures are inclusive by representing all aspects of society.

Have a trial run through to check your timings and have a contingency plan in case anything goes wrong, for example, a hard copy of an electronic presentation. Make sure you have all the necessary equipment, resources and stationery, and check in advance that everything is working. You may want to rearrange the area beforehand to suit your subject, and you will need to tidy up and clear the area at the end. Setting up and clearing away are outside of the observed time.

You should create and use a session plan which has a clear introduction, a middle section and an ending to your delivery.

The introduction

You may feel nervous as you will be observed; however, try and imagine you are *playing a role* and this should help your confidence. You are *the teacher* in this situation and must not let any personal issues interfere with this. Don't state that you are nervous as it probably won't show to your students. Speak a little more loudly and slowly than normal as being anxious or nervous may make you speak faster. If you feel you are shaking it is highly likely no one will notice this. If your mind suddenly goes blank, take a couple of deep breaths for a few seconds to help you refocus, it might seem a long time to you but it won't to your students. You will need to establish a rapport with your students, engage, interact and motivate them to make them feel at ease. Welcoming everyone to the session and stating your name is a nice way to start.

Keep your session plan handy as a prompt, ticking off aspects as you progress. If you feel you might forget something use a highlighter pen beforehand to mark key words which you can quickly see to prompt you. Introduce your aim and the objectives (you might like to keep these on display throughout your session – perhaps on a piece of flip chart paper on the wall, and refer to them as necessary). Use eye contact with all your students and use their names when possible. If you are writing on a board try and do this at an angle so as not to turn your back on the group. If you are using presentation software try not to have too much information on each slide, and look at the group as you talk through your points rather than at the screen. A *wireless slide presenter* is a useful gadget to have as it enables you to move around the room, clicking it to advance the slides, rather than standing next to the computer and tapping a key or using the mouse. Keep things simple, don't try to achieve too much yourself, or expect too much of your students. If this is the first time you have met your students, you might want to carry out a short icebreaker with them or ask them to introduce themselves to you. You may not have time to agree any ground rules; however, you could state that you expect mobile phones to be switched off. You should ask your students if they have any prior knowledge of the topic, if so you can draw on their experiences throughout your session. You might like to encourage your students to ask questions if they need to clarify any points and you could state that you will give a handout at the end which summarises your session.

The middle section

You should plan to use a variety of activities and appropriate teaching and learning approaches throughout your session. This will help engage your students, reach all learning styles and retain student motivation. Repeating important points will reinforce learning. This may be the first time your students have heard or seen something and repetition will help them remember. Summarise and recap regularly and ask open questions to check knowledge and understanding. Try and use names when talking to your students and include everyone in the group; don't just focus on a particular student whom you know can give you the correct answers. Open questions begin with who, what, when, where, why and how. Using closed questions, for example, 'are you all okay?' or 'do you have any questions?', will usually result in 'yes' or 'no' and does not help you ascertain their learning. As your students answer any questions, remember to acknowledge them and give constructive feedback. Always repeat the answers gained so that everyone in the group can hear them.

Try and vary your delivery and allow yourself time to explain points, followed by a written or practical activity for your students to carry out. This enables them to draw on their own knowledge and experience and to work together either in pairs or small groups to aid understanding. You need to manage all activities carefully and set a time limit for each, reminding them when the time is nearly up. Depending upon your students you could let them decide who they will work with; however, letting them decide for themselves may take up valuable time. You might like to plan ahead who will work with whom and be assertive when you state this. The timing of activities needs to be followed carefully, if you are only delivering a 15-minute session you may not have time for long group activities. If you do set activities, think what you will be doing whilst your students are working, and how long the activities will be. Moving around the room and the students shows an interest in what is happening, asking questions keeps them on track, and keeping an eye on the time shows you are managing the activity. Longer sessions benefit from a mixture of formal input from you, group activities, demonstrations and questions.

You will find the time will go really quickly, be prepared to adapt your timings if necessary, for example, if a group activity is going really well you could give your students a little longer. If your formal input is not being received well you could move onto an activity or a discussion. Have a spare activity or some open questions planned just in case you do have time to fill.

The ending

This is a summary of your aim and the objectives that have been covered in the session. You might like to ask your students if they have any questions; however, they may either be silent, or have lots of questions which will then impede upon your time. Issuing a handout is a good way of summarising the session content and will enable your students to read it afterwards. You could add useful text books and websites for students to research your topic further if they wish. Give the handout to your students at the end of the session as you summarise, otherwise they will be looking at it during the session which could cause disruption. A short quiz or multiple choice test is a good way to check knowledge if you have time and acts as an assessment activity. If you find you have covered everything and have spare time, you could ask each member of the group to state *one thing* they feel they have learnt from the session. This is a good way of filling in spare time if necessary, and shows you what has been learnt. You could also ask them to reflect on how they have met the aim of the session. If you are unsure of how to end your session, simply say 'thank you', this will indicate to your group and your observer that you have finished.

Do tidy the area when you finish, clean any boards you have used and close down any presentation equipment.

Level 4 micro-teach

If you are taking the PTLLS Award at level 4 you will need to demonstrate skills and knowledge appropriate with that level. For example, your session plan will need to be extremely detailed, follow a logical sequence and may need to show how you will embed literacy, language, numeracy and information communication technology (ICT). The individual needs of your students will need to be taken into account, for example, learning styles and different levels of ability. You should be aware of all the factors affecting your planning, delivery and assessment, such as student needs, the environment, resources and facilities, and also take into account equality and diversity, health and safety, and any relevant guidelines, codes of practice and legislation.

You should be able to deal with any situations as they arise, particularly regarding disruption and behaviour. A mixture of delivery styles, activities and assessment methods should be used to engage your students. Handouts should be of a high quality without any errors, and be issued at an appropriate time. There should be regular recaps to reinforce learning. You should demonstrate confidence of your subject and be able to answer any questions asked, communicating appropriately with everyone. Assessments should be varied and include open questions to each student allowing them all to participate. Feedback should be specific and developmental.

Verbal and non-verbal communication are both important. You should remain conscious of your body language and the way you speak, for example, voice projection and clarity, pace, language and jargon used. You need to remain focused and listen to your students, answering any questions as they arise. If you don't know the answer, say you will find out and make sure you do.

Using a variety of delivery methods and incorporating ICT, such as an interactive whiteboard, will demonstrate your skills at using equipment to its best effect to engage and motivate your students. You should be able to vary the timings of your activities to suit the flow of the session, group activities and individual needs.

Pre-service micro-teach

As a pre-service teacher you will be delivering to a group of your peers who will become your *students* for the session. You will probably be in the same environment you have been learning in, or a central meeting point if you have been studying through a distance learning programme. Hopefully you will have met your peers previously and feel comfortable delivering to them, if not it would be useful to talk to them beforehand to help everyone relax. Whilst your micro-teach will be in an environment that you are probably familiar with, it is essentially a simulation as you are not teaching real students. Even though it is a simulation, you may feel nervous and may have changed your mind a few times beforehand about what you will teach. Talk to your observer in advance about your ideas and once you have decided on a suitable topic try not to change your mind again but go ahead and prepare your session plan. You could show your session plan to your observer a few days prior to your delivery to gain appropriate feedback. Having a practice run-through at home with friends or family will help you plan your timings. You might also need to book some specialist equipment in advance or inform your peer group of anything they need to bring, for example, special clothing. You might want to check any prior knowledge of your peers in advance of the session or to inform them of the topic you will teach. You should have been told the date and time, how long your session should last and whether you will be visually recorded.

If you are due to deliver after someone else, you will probably be thinking about your own delivery rather than focusing upon theirs. Try not to do this as it might make you more nervous. Being well prepared, having knowledge of your topic and self-confidence should help you alleviate any worries.

Prior to your delivery, set up the area, check all equipment and move any tables and chairs as necessary (you might need help doing this) to ensure all your peers can see and hear you. Have a pen and your session plan somewhere close by to refer to regularly. A clock or a watch in a visible place will help you keep track of time. This should all be done prior to your session commencing. When you start, introduce yourself and your aim. You might like to ask if anyone has any prior knowledge of the subject you are delivering if you have not had the opportunity to do this beforehand. A useful question could be 'has anyone done this before?' This will help you include their experiences when asking questions and facilitating group activities. You may find your peers are very supportive during your micro-teach session and they might give you a round of applause at the end.

In-service micro-teach

You probably have some experience already of teaching, therefore delivering a session to your own students should be fairly straightforward. However, as you will be observed you may feel nervous or anxious.

Your session might last longer than the time your observer will be present, they might therefore miss the beginning or ending and arrive part way through. You should try and plan the session to allow time to talk to your observer either before or afterwards. This will enable you to discuss your delivery, to justify any aspects they have missed, and for you to receive feedback.

In preparation for your observed delivery, you might like to ask your subject mentor to observe one of your sessions and give you feedback. You could also observe your mentor or another colleague in the same subject area to see how they teach; you might pick up some useful ideas and information. Observing a teacher of a different subject to your own might give you some innovative ideas for your own subject.

The session you are delivering may be one of many, for which you will have a scheme of work to follow. You may want to introduce the observer to the group and state they are observing you, not them. Having a stranger in the room might lead to some behaviour issues. If so, you must deal with these as soon as they arise and in a professional manner. Your observer might be seeing the very first session of a programme, in which case you will have several administrative duties to perform, including an induction to the programme, icebreaker and the setting of ground rules. If you are being observed during one of several sessions, you will need to take the register and include a link to the last session with time for student questions during your introduction.

At the end of your session, you will need to link to the next session (if applicable) and set any additional work for higher level students. Before your students leave the room, make sure they tidy their work areas.

If this is the last session of a programme, you will need to incorporate some sort of evaluation activity to obtain feedback from your students regarding their experiences. Your organisation may have a standard pro-forma for this or you could design your own.

Giving and receiving feedback

Throughout your time attending a PTLLS Award programme you will have been carrying out various activities with your peers and giving each other feedback. You might have delivered some mini sessions and received feedback from your teacher as well as your peers. Sometimes, your peers may be more negative when giving you feedback as they are not yet as skilled as your teacher at being constructive. Try not to take any negative comments personally, your peers are just saying what they see, hopefully their feedback skills will improve as the programme progresses. Alternatively, you might feel the feedback from your peers is quite helpful. Feedback should always include something positive or constructive, as well as any areas for development.

One or more of your peers should give you feedback at the end of your observed micro-teach session. This might be verbal or written depending upon how much time there is.

Different feedback methods include:

- descriptive – gives examples of what could be improved and why, this can be written or verbal and is usually formal

- evaluative – statements such as *well done* or *good*. This method does not offer helpful or constructive advice; it can be written or verbal and is usually informal

Descriptive feedback lets you describe *what* has been done, *how* it has been achieved and *what* needs to be done to progress further. It enables you to provide opportunities for students to make any adjustments or improvements to reach a particular standard.

Evaluative feedback might be good to hear, for example, 'well done Pete'; however, it does not give the student any opportunity to know *what* was done well or *how* they could improve.

Giving feedback

Giving feedback is a part of achieving the PTLLS Award and you may find it hard to do at first. You will be giving feedback during your micro-teach session to your students (real or peers). You may also be required to give feedback to your peers for their micro-teach sessions.

When giving feedback to others you need to be aware it could affect their self-esteem and whether they continue with the programme or not. The quality of feedback received can be a key factor in their progress and the ability to learn new skills. Ongoing constructive feedback which has been carefully thought through is an indication of your interest in the person and of your intention to help them develop and do well in the future.

When giving feedback:

- own your statements by using the word 'I' rather than 'you'

- begin with something positive, for example, '*I really liked the confident manner in which you delivered your session*'

- you could then ask the person how they felt their session went, i.e. what were their strengths and areas for development. They may have noticed some aspects which need improvement, if so, this saves you having to be too critical

- be specific about what you have seen, for example, '*I felt the way you explained your topic was really interesting due to your knowledge and humour*' or '*I found the way you explained your topic was rather confusing to me*'

- offer constructive, specific or developmental follow-on points, for example, '*I feel I would have understood it better if you had broken the subject down into smaller stages*'

- end with something positive, for example, '*I enjoyed your session, you had prepared well and came across as very organised and professional*'.

Being constructive, specific and developmental with what you say, and owning your statements should help the person focus upon what you are saying as they will hear how they can improve. If you don't have any constructive, specific or developmental follow-on points then don't create them just for the sake of it. Conversely, if you do have any negative points or criticisms, don't say '*my only negative point is...*' or '*my only criticisms are...*'. It's much better to replace these words and say '*some areas for development could be...*'.

You also need to make sure you are not being ambiguous or vague, you need to be factual regarding what you have seen and heard, not just give your personal opinion. Bear in mind that what you say can help or hinder a person's progress and confidence. Starting with something positive will help their motivation; they are then likely to listen to what else you have to say, which will aid their development. Starting with something negative can be demoralising and they may not listen to what else is said. Negative comments can have a more powerful impact than positive ones even though they are not nice to hear. If you do need to give negative feedback, always back this up with specific suggestions as to how the person can improve.

Feedback should be a two-way process, allowing a discussion to take place to clarify any points. Consider your tone of voice and take into account any non-verbal signals, you may need to adapt your feedback if you see someone is becoming uncomfortable. Be aware of your own body language, facial expressions and tone of voice and don't use confrontational words or words likely to cause offence.

Not every individual in the peer group will give feedback after each micro-teach session. Depending upon the amount of time, one person might give verbal feedback and the others will give written feedback.

If you are writing your feedback, this will probably be read at a later time; therefore you need to appreciate that *how* you write it may not be how it is read. It is easy to interpret words or phrases differently to those intended. Statements such as *well done* or *good* don't say *what* was *well done* or *good* or how it can be improved for the future. However, statements such as *your use of the technology was very effective and demonstrated the point very well – well done* make the feedback more explicit.

The feedback you are giving is only your opinion, the observer will also be giving feedback and should clarify any points you have raised to ensure the person you have given feedback to does not feel demoralised. He or she may also give you feedback on how you have given feedback to your peers, to help you improve your own skills. If you can give feedback in a skilful manner, the others in the room will also learn from and benefit by what you have said. Peer assessment and constructive feedback has a valuable contribution to make to everyone's learning and development within the group.

Your observer should have planned who will be giving feedback to whom to enable everyone to focus carefully upon the relevant individual's session.

Receiving feedback

Once you have finished your micro-teach session, you might be so relieved or busy packing away that you don't fully take on board what is being said to you. Listen carefully and ask questions to clarify any points you are unsure of. Try not to interrupt or become defensive when receiving feedback and don't take anything personally, the feedback will be given to help you improve.

Receiving feedback can sometimes be difficult as people often think it will be negative or critical. If one of your peers gives you negative feedback you might feel your self-esteem is in question and want to be defensive or argumentative. If this happens, listen to what they say, but remember it is their opinion and your observer will also give you feedback which may differ from this. Just say 'I'll take your comments on board' rather than arguing. Conversely, you might receive really good feedback and not know how to react. If this is the case, simply say 'thank you for your comments'.

When receiving feedback, whether from your peers or observer, you need to listen carefully, focusing on the positive as well as any negative or constructive points. The feedback from your observer should be given skilfully to help you realise what you did well and what you could improve upon for the future to reach your full potential.

You should receive a completed feedback form from your observer as well as from your peers, these can be used to inform your self-evaluation process.

Evaluating your micro-teach session

After delivering your micro-teach session, you should reflect on how you felt it went, this will aid your self-evaluation process. Evaluating your own delivery is an important aspect of your learning and development. You might think you have done really well, but others may have given you some helpful advice during the feedback process which could improve your future teaching and personal development. You may even have received comments you had not considered and can therefore use these to help you improve or change things.

If your session has been visually recorded, you should view this as soon as possible and read your observer's feedback and peer feedback forms to help you evaluate how your session went. The forms and recording media can be placed in your portfolio as evidence of achievement.

When evaluating yourself, consider your strengths, areas for development and any action and improvements required from a teaching perspective as well as your subject knowledge.

Some questions to ask yourself include:

- how did I feel after I delivered my session?

- did I achieve my aim?

- what are my strengths and areas for development?

- did I deliver within the time or did I have to adjust/change anything?

- did I engage all my students throughout the session?

- how do I know if everyone learnt something?

- how effective were the teaching/learning approaches I used?

- did anything go wrong – if so what did I do or could I do in the future to ensure this does not happen again?

- how did my session meet the needs of the group and individuals?

- what would I do differently next time?

- how can I use the feedback received to improve for the future?

Micro-teaching hints and tips

You might find the following hints and tips useful to help you focus on the micro-teaching process.

- Prepare your session plan in advance, ensuring you have an aim and SMART objectives, and that you have a beginning, middle and end to your delivery.

- Try not to change your mind too many times about what to teach.

- Keep things simple – don't try to achieve too much.

- Practise your session at home in front of friends/family; they may ask questions which will help you plan your responses.

- Check your timings are realistic, have an extra activity in case you have spare time, or know what you can leave out if you run short of time.

- Arrive early to check the room, equipment and resources.

- Set up the area to suit your topic, so that everyone can see and hear you – you might need to move tables, chairs and equipment.

- Be prepared, be organised, be professional and dress appropriately for your subject.

- Have a watch handy, or position a clock somewhere so that you can keep track of the time, have spare pens, paper, board marker, etc.

- Have a contingency plan in case anything goes wrong or is not available, for example, handouts as an alternative just in case the presentation equipment stops working.

- Introduce yourself, your aim and the objectives, it is useful to have these visible throughout your session perhaps on flip chart paper – check with your observer if you need to use an icebreaker or agree ground rules.

- Present your topic confidently and include the group with questions and short activities, make use of resources such as ICT/board/flip chart/projector and/or presentation software.

- Check slides and handouts for spelling/grammar/punctuation errors and ensure text and pictures represent all aspects of society.

- Use names when speaking to individuals or asking questions.

- Use eye contact and stand tall, speak a little slower and louder than normal.

- If you set a group activity, think about what you will be doing whilst they are active, and set time limits.

- Check learning has taken place by asking open questions or carrying out some form of assessment activity, for example, a worksheet or quiz, always confirm achievement (or otherwise) and give constructive feedback.

- It is useful to provide a handout to summarise your session with further details, for example, books, websites, etc.

- Recap your aim and objectives in your summary.

- If you are not sure what to do when you finish simply say 'thank you'.

- Tidy up afterwards.

Summary

In this chapter you have learnt about:

- planning and preparing your micro-teach session

- giving and receiving feedback

- evaluating your micro-teach session

- micro-teaching hints and tips

Theory focus

References and further information

Gravells, A (2012) *Preparing to Teach in the Lifelong Learning Sector: The New Award* (5th Edn). London: Learning Matters.

Reece, I and Walker, S (2007) *Teaching, Training and Learning; A Practical Guide* (6th Edn). Tyne & Wear: Business Education Publishers Ltd.

Wallace, S (2011) *Teaching, Tutoring and Training in the Lifelong Learning Sector* (4th Edn). Exeter: Learning Matters.

Williams, J (2012) *Study Skills for your PTLLS* (2nd Edn). London: Learning Matters.

Websites

Giving feedback – http://www.brookes.ac.uk/services/ocsld/firstwords/fw21.html

Abbreviations and Acronyms

ACE	Adult and Continuing Education
ACL	Adult and Community Learning
ADS	Adult Dyslexia Support
ALN	Adult Literacy and Numeracy
AO	Awarding Organisation
ATLS	Associate Teacher Learning and Skills
BIS	Business Innovation and Skills
BSA	Basic Skills Agency
CCEA	Council for the Curriculum, Examinations and Assessment (Northern Ireland)
Cert Ed	Certificate of Education
CIEA	Chartered Institute of Educational Assessors
COSHH	Control of Substances Hazardous to Health
CPD	Continuing professional development
CTLLS	Certificate in Teaching in the Lifelong Learning Sector
DCELLS	Department for Children, Education, Lifelong Learning and Skills (Wales)
DfE	Department for Education
DTLLS	Diploma in Teaching in the Lifelong Learning Sector
DSO	Designated Safeguarding Officer
ECM	Every Child Matters
EDAR	Experience, describe, analyse and revise
EI	Emotional intelligence
EQA	External quality assurer
GCSE	General Certificate of Secondary Education
GLH	Guided Learning Hours
IAG	Initial advice and guidance
ICT	Information Communication Technology
IfL	Institute for Learning
ILP	Individual Learning Plan
ILT	Information Learning Technology
ITT	Initial Teacher Training
IQ	Intelligence Quotient

IQA	Internal quality assurer
LAR	Learner Achievement Record
LLN	Language, Literacy, Numeracy
LSIS	Learning and Skills Improvement Service
NLP	Neuro Linguistic Programming
NOS	National Occupational Standards
NVQ	National Vocational Qualification
Ofqual	Office of Qualifications and Examinations Regulation
Ofsted	Office for Standards in Education, Children's Services and Skills
OHP	Overhead projector
PCET	Post Compulsory Education and Training
PGCE	Post Graduate Certificate in Education
PPP	Pose, pause, pounce
PTLLS	Preparing to Teach in the Lifelong Learning Sector
QCF	Qualifications and Credit Framework
QTLS	Qualified Teacher Learning and Skills
RLJ	Reflective Learning Journal
RPL	Recognition of prior learning
RWE	Realistic working environment
SCN	Scottish candidate number
SfA	Skills Funding Agency
SMART	Specific, measurable, achievable, realistic and time
SQF	Scottish Qualifications Framework
SSB	Standard Setting Body
SSC	Sector Skills Council
SWOT	Strengths, weaknesses, opportunities and threats
TAQA	Training, assessment and quality assurance
ULN	Unique learner number
VACSR	Valid, authentic, current, sufficient and reliable
VARK	Visual, aural, read/write and kinaesthetic
VLE	Virtual learning environment
WBL	Work Based Learning
WWWWWH	Who, what, when, where, why and how
YPLA	Young People's Learning Agency

Glossary of Terms

Term	Definition
Activity	a short task designed to enable students to consolidate their learning
Action Plan	formal agreement between a teacher and student agreeing what will be achieved and when
Aim	general statement outlining what the teacher hopes to achieve
Assessment	a way of finding out if learning has taken place
Assessment criteria	statements used in the QCF to determine what students can do
Assessment cycle	the full process of assessment from beginning to end
Assessment method	a way of finding out if learning has taken place, e.g. assignment, observation, questions, etc.
Assessment type	style of assessment, e.g. initial, formative, summative, etc.
Assessor	person responsible for making a decision as to a student's achievements
Associate teacher	a person performing the role required for ATLS, i.e. having less responsibility than a full teacher and usually teaching from materials prepared by others
Authentic	the student's own work
Award	a term used in the QCF to denote a qualification with 12 credits or less
Awarding organisation	an organisation recognised by the Ofqual for the purpose of awarding qualifications
Barriers to learning	concerns or issues that could hinder learning taking place, e.g. transport, English as a second language, etc.
Boundaries	restrictions affecting the teaching role
Certificate	a term used in the QCF to denote a qualification with 13–36 credits
Communication	the transfer of information, from one person to another, with the intention of bringing about a response
Contact time	time spent in contact with a teacher or assessor

Diagnostic assessment	a way of ascertaining a student's current skills and knowledge towards a particular subject
Differentiation	recognising differences in people or something
Diploma	a term used in the QCF to denote a qualification with 37 or more credits
Diversity	valuing individual differences
Engage	encouraging student interaction with the teacher and others
Environment	anywhere learning takes place
Equality	having equal rights
Evaluation	measuring the effectiveness of a session or a programme of learning
Evidence	proof of achievement, e.g. written statements, work products, etc.
External quality assurer	person accountable to the awarding body who ensures quality assurance by monitoring and advising internal verifiers and assessors
Feedback	information to confirm achievement or to motivate a student to learn further
Full teacher	a person performing the role required for QTLS, i.e. having more responsibility than an associate teacher
Ground rules	agreed codes of behaviour between the teacher and the student. Usually agreed at the beginning of the programme, e.g. non-use of mobile phones
Holistic	covering several aspects at the same time
Icebreaker	fun and lighthearted ways of introducing students to each other
Inclusive	involving everyone, treating them equally and fairly
Initial assessment	assessment carried out at the beginning of a programme or session
In-service	currently in a teaching role
Interactive whiteboard	an electronic board used to display information and presentations which can be connected to the internet

Internal quality assurer	a person accountable to the external verifier and City & Guilds who is based in the approved centre and who co-ordinates assessment arrangements and monitors assessor standards
Learning outcome	statements used in the QCF to determine what students will do
Learning styles	a particular way in which an individual prefers to learn, e.g. visual, aural, read/write and kinaesthetic (VARK)
Level	a measure of the demand of a qualification. QCF levels start at Entry and go up to 8 in England (12 in Scotland)
Mentor	person giving one-to-one support who is skilled and/or knowledgeable in the same subject area
Micro-teach	a formal delivery of a session to a peer group
Minimum core	literacy, language, numeracy and ICT – the minimum skills a teacher should demonstrate
Motivation	factors influencing a student's learning, e.g. intrinsic – the desire to learn for own self fulfilment, and/or extrinsic – external factors such as a pay rise at work or the achievement of a qualification
Non-contact time	time spent not in contact with a teacher or assessor, i.e. for studies, assignment work, research, etc.
Non-verbal communication	any communication that does not involve the spoken word, e.g. body language, facial expression
Objective	ways in which students can achieve an aim, e.g. by demonstrating, describing or explaining, etc.
Peer assessment	assessment by other students or colleagues in the same group
Plagiarism	copying the work of someone else without acknowledging the source
Points of referral	people or places to refer a student to if necessary
Powerpoint	a computer program used to present teaching and learning materials
Pre-service	not yet in a teaching role
Qualification	a formally recognised programme of learning

Qualifications and credit framework (QCF)	a system for recognising skills and qualifications (SCQF in Scotland)
Qualitative	quality information obtained by open questions, reports and discussions
Quality Assurance	organisational procedures (internal and external) to ensure standards are maintained
Quantitative	quantity information, e.g. data and statistics obtained by closed questions, results from tests and other data gathering techniques
Records	documents used to support the teaching and learning process which satisfy internal and external requirements
Reflection	thinking about what has occurred, what can be improved and why
Reliable	consistent
Resources	materials used to enhance the learning process, e.g. handouts, computers, text books, audio visual equipment, etc.
Scheme of Work	an outline of what will be covered during a programme
Self-assessment	assessment by the student
Session Plan	an outline of what will be covered during a session
Student	a person taking a learning programme
Teacher	generic term for trainer, tutor, instructor, facilitator, lecturer who enables learning to take place
Teaching and learning approaches, strategies and techniques	methods of facilitating learning, e.g. discussion, e-learning, presentation, project, group work, etc.
Teaching and learning cycle	systematic approach to teaching and learning in five stages: identifying needs, planning learning, facilitating learning, assessing learning, and quality assurance and evaluation
Unit	part of a full qualification, i.e. a small chunk of learning
Valid	suitable